"Here is the voice of historic Christianity speaking about Christian assurance with clarity, wisdom, and grace and doing so at a time of enormous cultural uncertainty, drift, and self-doubt. The importance of the issue and the excellence of its treatment here alike commend this book." —**David F. Wells**

"If you are ever tempted to doubt that the assurance of God's love is one of the benefits of justification, here is an excellent antidote. This book will set you on the path to security, stability, and joyful discipleship." —**Alistair Begg**

"Assurance of God's gracious, saving, fatherly love to us in Christ is vital to Christian life and witness. Unfortunately, too many saints lack assurance, and today there are even Reformed and evangelical preachers who are undermining it by erroneous teaching. Thankfully a band of faithful brothers has given us this book to clear the fog, present the truth, and help us on our way. Read this book prayerfully, with faith in God's Word, and be encouraged!" —**J. Ligon Duncan III**

"Thank you, Burk, for such a clear, thorough, and easy-to-understand book on what the Bible has to say about the assurance of salvation. For those who have questions, this will give them the answers!" —**Joni Eareckson Tada**

"The leadership of Burk Parsons has effectively brought together pastors, theologians, and authors who are not only adept at ministry but competent to address the issue of divine assurance in a personal relationship with Christ. Now we have an effective tool that will assist pastors ~~and Christians~~ ~~~~ ~~~~ eir disciple-making ministry." —

Assured by God

LIVING IN THE FULLNESS
OF GOD'S GRACE

*Second Edition,
with Study Questions*

Edited by
Burk Parsons

PUBLISHING
P.O. BOX 817 • PHILLIPSBURG • NEW JERSEY 08865-0817

Page design and typesetting by Lakeside Design Plus

Printed in the United States of America

Library of Congress Control Number: 2007935320

Contents

Contents

FOREWORD

R. C. Sproul

The full assurance of salvation is not an extra benefit that ac-
crues only to those believers who have striven mightily to reach
a higher level of sanctification. Rather, assurance is a gracious
gift of God provided for us in salvation and is to be secured
early in our Christian lives. In his second epistle, Peter writes:
"Therefore, brothers, be all the more diligent to make your
calling and election sure, for if you practice these qualities you
will never fall. For in this way there will be richly provided
for you an entrance into the eternal kingdom of our Lord and
Savior Jesus Christ" (2 Peter 1:10–11). This exhortation follows
on the heels of Peter's call for Christians to manifest the fruit
of the Spirit, in a manner similar to the way the apostle Paul
urged Christians to manifest the fruit of the Spirit. The key to
fruitfulness, the key to manifesting a productive Christian life,
is to have a life that is founded solidly on the assurance of one's
salvation in Christ. The unsure Christian is the Christian who
lacks stability in his or her faith. The unsure Christian is tossed
to and fro with every wind of doctrine. The unsure Christian
is easy prey for the assault of Satan, who does everything in his

malevolent power to undermine the Christian's confidence of salvation in Christ. A Christian who lacks such confidence can easily become trapped in insecurity and may lack the boldness to venture out into the domain of a fallen world, armed with the whole armor of God. The pages of this book are designed to help Christians understand the true nature of the assurance of salvation so that they might grow in their own confidence of what God has wrought in them. It is my prayer that those who read this volume will have those vacillating doubts that weaken their profession removed once and for all, so that they may be fully equipped to be fruit bearers in the vineyard of Christ.

It is of vital importance not only to have true assurance but to have a sound understanding of what true assurance contains. It is all too easy for people to gain a false confidence of their salvation. Nothing is deadlier than for a person to have a false security—being at ease in Zion—assuming that one is in a state of grace and salvation while in reality one is still far from the kingdom. The difference between authentic faith and counterfeit faith must be understood if the assurance we possess is to be valid. In our day, many people have been evangelized with techniques that convince them that if they make a profession of faith they are therefore saved. It is critical, however, to understand that justification is not by mere profession of faith, but by the actual possession of that faith we profess. Assurance based merely upon action taken at an evangelistic meeting or upon the signing of a commitment card is an unstable kind of assurance that must be examined carefully to validate its foundation. Full assurance of faith comes from the Holy Spirit through the Word of God. Throughout this book the foundational principles of the Word of God are set forth, for it is only by the Word of God that we can learn to discern the difference between spurious faith and saving faith, between authentic assurance and its counterfeit.

Assurance in its authentic state is related to a biblical understanding of how salvation is received. The doctrine of assurance never stands alone. It must always be joined with our understanding of the elements of justification and our understanding of the way in which we appropriate the benefits of the ministry of Christ to our lives. The whole counsel of God comes to bear in our quest for genuine assurance. It is an assurance based upon the word of promise given to God's people that Christ redeems us when we place real faith in a real Savior, trusting in his righteousness and his righteousness alone. When we do this, we are moving in the direction we need to go to gain the full assurance of salvation.

The possession of full assurance of salvation is too important to leave to a superficial search. It must be an earnest quest, fueled by the impetus of the Holy Spirit who impels our souls to seek the truth of our own condition, in that truth that God reveals to us in sacred Scripture. May your journey in pursuit of full assurance be guided at every step by the unvarnished Word of God, by God's grace and for his glory.

PREFACE

Burk Parsons

Just as our Lord instills humility within our minds, so he establishes assurance within our hearts. Not only does the Lord conquer our rebellious hearts and make us surrender to him as our king, he bestows upon us one of the most precious of all spiritual blessings in Christ—the assurance of salvation. Although many have unwisely presumed otherwise, assurance of salvation does not flow from a proud heart that boasts of one's ability to maintain a bold profession of faith. On the contrary, God assures us of our salvation in Christ precisely because our hearts have been broken and humbled by God himself, for it is on account of his ability to maintain his bold possession of our souls that we have assurance. He assures us not by giving us confidence in ourselves but by bringing us to the end of ourselves so that we might know and love him. That is the pure brilliance of the glorious gospel of Christ. At every point in our lives, and with every blessed act of divine discipline, God's strength is made perfect in our weakness.

Our problem is that we want others to see how strong we are. We do not want people, especially other Christians, to see our weaknesses. We want both the church and the world to see just how perfect we have become, and most of us certainly do not want to be seen reading a book on the assurance of salvation. Nevertheless, many people who sit in the pews of evangelical churches throughout the world do not possess full assurance of their salvation. When trials come into their lives, many Christians find themselves doubting their salvation, doubting the imputed righteousness of Christ, doubting God's sovereignty, and doubting the grace of God instead of fleeing to their loving Father's arms. In this fallen world of despair and doubt, with minds and hearts that have been corrupted by sin, every Christian needs to understand fully the promises that the Lord God Almighty has established for us and within us. He has promised us that we are his children, he has promised us a glorious inheritance in Christ, and he has poured out his love within our hearts by the Holy Spirit.

No doctrine of God's Word is to be taken lightly, and the biblical doctrine of assurance is not a subject to be studied casually. It is precisely because the doctrine of assurance has been treated with such flippancy and neglect that this book has been written. In the 1870s J. C. Ryle wrote on the believer's assurance of salvation in his classic work *Holiness*. The words he penned are certainly appropriate today, and the contributors of this book echo his wise remarks:

> I shall [consider one point] the more readily, because of the great importance which attaches to the subject of assurance, and the great neglect with which, I humbly conceive, it is often treated in this day. But I shall do it at the same time with fear and trembling. I feel that I am treading on very difficult ground, and that it is easy to speak rashly and unscripturally in this matter. The road between truth and error

is here a specially narrow pass; and if I shall be enabled to do good to some without doing harm to others, I shall be very thankful.[1]

The authors who contributed to this book did so on account of their earnest desire to help Christian laypeople understand the character and nature of God's promises to them. Therefore, we write with pastoral concern for God's people, and it is our prayer that God would use the fallible words of this book to direct his people to the truths of his infallible Word.

CONTRIBUTORS

Joel R. Beeke is president and professor of systematic theology and homiletics at Puritan Reformed Theological Seminary, pastor of the Heritage Netherlands Reformed Congregation in Grand Rapids, Michigan, editor of *Banner of Sovereign Grace Truth*, editorial director of Reformation Heritage Books, president of Inheritance Publishers, and vice president of the Dutch Reformed Translation Society. He has written or edited fifty books and contributed more than fifteen hundred articles to Reformed books, journals, periodicals, and encyclopedias. His PhD is in Reformation and post-Reformation theology from Westminster Theological Seminary. He is frequently called upon to lecture at seminaries and to speak at Reformed conferences around the world. He and his wife Mary have been blessed with three children.

Jerry Bridges is an author and Bible teacher. His most popular title, *The Pursuit of Holiness*, has sold more than one million copies. He has authored several other books, including *The Discipline of Grace*, *Transforming Grace*, and *The Gospel for Real*

Life. He is currently part of the Navigator collegiate ministry group, in which he is involved in staff development and serves as a resource to campus ministries.

Sinclair B. Ferguson is professor of systematic theology at Westminster Seminary in Dallas, Texas, and is recognized as one of the world's leading Reformed scholars. He serves as senior pastor of First Presbyterian Church (ARP) in Columbia, South Carolina, and has served as an associate editor for the Banner of Truth Trust since 1976. He has authored many books, including *The Christian Life*, *The Big Book of Questions and Answers*, and *The Holy Spirit*.

John MacArthur has been since 1969 the pastor-teacher of Grace Community Church in Sun Valley, California, where he labors to equip believers through the systematic exposition of the Bible. His teaching ministry can be heard worldwide on the radio program "Grace to You" and through some twelve million teaching tapes. He is currently president of the Master's College and Seminary and has authored numerous books, including *The Gospel according to Jesus*, *The Battle for the Beginning*, and *Follow Me*.

Keith A. Mathison is associate editor of *Tabletalk* magazine. He received his MA from Reformed Theological Seminary and his PhD from Whitefield Theological Seminary. He is the editor of *When Shall These Things Be?* and author of *Dispensationalism*, *Postmillennialism*, *The Shape of Sola Scriptura*, and *Given for You*.

R. Albert Mohler Jr. serves as the ninth president of the Southern Baptist Theological Seminary and hosts a daily radio program for the Salem Radio Network. He earned his BA from Samford

University and his MDiv and PhD from Southern Seminary. He serves as professor of Christian theology at Southern Seminary. He has contributed to several books, including *Hell under Fire: Modern Scholarship Reinvents Eternal Punishment*, *Here We Stand: A Call from Confessing Evangelicals*, and *The Coming Evangelical Crisis*. He currently serves as editor-in-chief of *The Southern Baptist Journal of Theology*. He is married to the former Mary Kahler; they have two children.

Burk Parsons serves as minister of congregational life at Saint Andrew's Chapel in Sanford, Florida, and is the editor of *Tabletalk*, the monthly Bible study magazine of Ligonier Ministries. He holds a degree in biblical studies from Trinity College and the MDiv from Reformed Theological Seminary. He and his wife, Amber, live in Longwood, Florida, with their children.

Richard D. Phillips serves as senior minister of First Presbyterian Church in Margate, Florida. He serves on the board of directors of the Alliance of Confessing Evangelicals, and he chairs the Philadelphia Conference on Reformed Theology, founded by the late James Montgomery Boice, his mentor and former pastor. He has written several books, including *Faith Victorious*, *Turning Back the Darkness*, and *Holding Hands, Holding Hearts*, which he coauthored with his wife, Sharon. They and their five children live in Cape Coral, Florida.

Philip Graham Ryken is senior minister of Tenth Presbyterian Church in Philadelphia. He is a council member of the Alliance of Confessing Evangelicals and is the author of several books, including *City on a Hill*, *The Message of Salvation*, and *The Doctrines of Grace*, cowritten with his predecessor James Montgomery Boice. He and his wife, Elisabeth, live in the Philadelphia area with their five children.

R. C. Sproul serves as minister of preaching and teaching at Saint Andrew's Chapel in Sanford, Florida. He is the founder and chairman of Ligonier Ministries. He holds degrees from Westminster College, Pittsburgh Theological Seminary, the Free University of Amsterdam, and Whitefield Theological Seminary. He has written more than sixty books, including *Scripture Alone*, *The Intimate Marriage*, and the classic *The Holiness of God*.

1

OUR SURE FOUNDATION

Burk   Parsons

> Assurance . . . is a thing that is above the capacity of the human mind, it is the part of the Holy Spirit to confirm within us what God promises in his Word.
>
> —John Calvin, *Commentary on 2 Corinthians*

"We need a liberty fortified and confirmed by the gift of perseverance, so that we may overcome this world, with all its loves, its fears, and its errors." Toward the end of his life, Augustine penned these simple words that help us understand the profound majesty of our assurance of salvation (*On Rebuke and Grace* 35). Whether we want to admit it, we all struggle to overcome the world (John 16:33; 1 John 5:4), and we all struggle to enjoy the glorious freedoms we have in Christ (John 8:32). Many of our struggles exist because we do not fully understand that just as our salvation is a gift from God, so our perseverance is a gift from God. In our salvation, God blesses us with assurance through his gift of perseverance (2 Thessalonians 3:5). However, many Christians lack full assurance of their salvation because their understanding of assurance is founded on the constantly changing emotions of their hearts rather than on the eternal Word of God.

The Assurance of Our Perseverance

Many Christians who are members of Bible-preaching, evangelical churches have been duped somehow into thinking that their perseverance in the faith is dependent on their own natural abilities to endure to the end. They have become practical deists, thinking that after God made us a new creation (2 Corinthians 5:17) he simply left us to our own devices while he just sits back observing us through life's difficulties, waiting to see if we will make it to the end.

In his first wartime address, delivered at Guildhall in London on September 4, 1914, Sir Winston Churchill (1874–1965) said: "Sure I am of this, that you have only to endure to conquer. You have only to persevere to save yourselves." Considering what Churchill accomplished during his life, he proved this statement to be entirely appropriate. The British Prime Minister's wartime victories demonstrated time and again his ability to persevere to the end. He overcame great odds, and his self-sustained resilience enabled him to endure all the struggles of leadership during the Second World War. And while his assertion is accurate, it is accurate only insofar as it pertains to our natural human abilities. Churchill's call to persevere in order to save oneself is by all means applicable to soldiers in wartime. It is a stern charge to fight to the end in order to overcome the enemy. Moreover, it conveys a similar exhortation found in the Bible. In Hebrews, we are called to run the race set before us (12:1). The apostle Paul likewise admonishes us to endure so that we might "reign with [Christ]" (2 Timothy 2:12). And while teaching his disciples, Christ himself said: "The one who endures to the end will be saved" (Matthew 10:22). In these passages and others, the Bible's teaching is clear; we must persevere to the end in order to be saved. However, this is only one part of the biblical equation. If our perseverance in the faith is dependent upon us, we will surely fail and will by no means finish the race set before us. Moreover, our assurance of salvation will waver each and every day if we are counting on ourselves and our own natural abilities to persevere to the end (Romans 4:20; Hebrews 10:23). In order to have full assurance, we must be entirely dependent upon Christ and his Word, which he has provided for us as our only infallible rule for faith and life (Westminster Confession of Faith 1.2). In his letter to the Colossians, the apostle Paul writes to the saints and faithful believers in Christ at Colossae:

> For I want you to know how great a struggle I have for you and for those at Laodicea and for all who have not seen me face to face, that their hearts may be encouraged, being knit together in love, to reach all the riches of full assurance of understanding and the knowledge of God's mystery, which is Christ, in whom are hidden all the treasures of wisdom and knowledge. (Colossians 2:1–3)

The Foundation of Assurance

As Christians, we have not been left to our own devices "to reach all the riches of full assurance of understanding and the knowledge of God's mystery," nor have we been left to figure out for ourselves all that God requires of us. We have been blessed with the wisdom and knowledge of our Savior, Jesus Christ, for in him "are hidden all the treasures of wisdom and knowledge" (Colossians 2:3). What is more, in his sovereign wisdom God provided us with his Word; by his sovereign grace he provided us with minds to comprehend the treasures of wisdom and knowledge in his Word; and as a loving Father, he provided us with hearts to love and obey his Word. We are a people who are identified as God's people because we are a people who are identified by his Word. We have been called to hide the Word in our hearts so that we might not sin against the Lord (Psalm 119:11), and we have been told to allow "the word of Christ [to] dwell in [us] richly, teaching and admonishing one another in all wisdom, singing psalms and hymns and spiritual songs, with thankfulness in [our] hearts to God" (Colossians 3:16). The Word of God is not only true and it does not merely contain truth, it is truth; that is to say, it defines truth (John 17:17).

However, many people are under the impression that the Word of God is merely a gospel tract to explain how to get a fire ticket out of hell and how to receive a golden pass so that we can get into heaven. What is more, some people think that the Bible is a step-by-step manual on how to be a nice person and how to live the good life. As such, many people keep their Bibles on their shelves and look at them only when they find themselves in serious trouble; for them, the Word of God is a big book of stories, poems, and facts that looks nice on the coffee table. But as John Piper writes in his classic book *Desiring God*, the Word of God is much more than that: "So the Bible is the Word of God. And the Word of God is no trifle. It is the source of faith and life and power and hope and freedom and wisdom and comfort and assurance and victory over our greatest enemy."[1] The Westminster Larger Catechism explains that the Word is a means of God's grace to his people:

The Spirit of God maketh the reading, but especially the preaching of the word, an effectual means of enlightening, convincing, and humbling sinners; of driving them out of themselves, and drawing them unto Christ; of conforming them to his image, and subduing them to his will; of strengthening them against temptations and corruptions; of building them up in grace, and establishing their hearts in holiness and comfort through faith unto salvation. (A. 155)

Some Christians have studied the Word of God for many years. They know their Bibles backward and forward, and they know every doctrinal "i" that should be dotted and every systematic "t" that should be crossed. They love the theology of the Word of God, but their love for God himself has been displaced (Isaiah 29:13). This can happen in many ways. Whether it is our love of spending time studying things about God or whether it is our love of spending time serving God, such things can too easily replace our love for God himself who is our great reward, our everlasting inheritance (Genesis 15:1; Joshua 13:14).

When I was nineteen years old, I joined the staff of a large evangelical church. Many of the pastors on the staff became wonderful friends and mentors, but as I encountered some of the pastors at that church and at churches in the area, I became deeply saddened by what I observed. As I got to know some of the pastors more intimately, I observed that their love for the ministry seemed to supersede their love for God. It appeared that over the years, the ministry had become their god.

In his best-selling book *The Man in the Mirror*, Patrick Morley underscores the reality of this problem in the following story: "Ron Jensen rented a travel camper and traveled around the country with his wife while working on his doctoral thesis. His task was to interview 350 Christian leaders. At the end of this tour he made a discouraging observation. He said, 'I found a great deal of zeal for God's work, but very little passion for God.'"[2]

As a student in Bible college, preparing for service in the church, it scared me to death to think that I could someday get to the point that my love for the ministry might take the place of my love for God. Therefore, every year since then I have dedicated myself to God, asking him to help me live for him and not for the ministry alone. In his boldly prophetic and now manifestly appropriate book *The Church at the End of the Twentieth Century*, Francis Schaeffer helps to illustrate the importance of doctrinal faithfulness, not as an end in itself, but as the means to loving God rightly:

> We must ask, "Do I fight merely for doctrinal faithfulness?" This is like the wife who never sleeps with anybody else, but never shows love to her own husband. Is that a sufficient relationship in marriage? No, ten thousand times no. Yet if I am a Christian who speaks and acts for doctrinal faithfulness but do not show love to my divine bridegroom, I am in the same place as such a wife. What God wants from us is not only doctrinal faithfulness, but our love day by day. Not in theory, mind you, but in practice.
>
> For those of us who are the children of God, there can be only one end to this study concerning adultery and apostasy. We must realize the seriousness of modern apostasy; we must urge each other not to have any part in modern apostasy. But at the same time we must realize that we must love our Savior and Lord. We must be the loving, true bride of the divine bridegroom in reality and in practice, day by day, in the midst of the spiritual adultery of our day. Our call is first to be the bride faithful, but that is not the total call. The call is not only to be the bride faithful, but to be the bride in love.[3]

As the people of God, we cannot let our love for the things concerning God replace our love for God himself. Rather, we must be consumed with the understanding that all of our service to God and all of our understanding about God should lead us to love God more and more. Our study of God and our service to God that is accomplished for God's glory and for the good of his people should lead us to love God. In the preface of his book *The Holy Spirit*, Sinclair Ferguson quotes Thomas Aquinas as having taught that theology proceeds from God, teaches us about God, and leads us to God (*theologia deum docet, ab deo docetur, ad deum ducit*).[4] The theology of the Word of God teaches us about God, but the process does not end there. What we learn about God from his Word teaches us how to serve him, how to love him, and how to worship him. If our service to God and our knowledge about God do not lead us to love God and praise God, then it could be said that ultimately we do not know the God of the Bible. Consider again Colossians 3:16: if the word of Christ indwells us richly, we will not be able to help but praise God with thankful hearts.

Being a Christian is not just about knowing things about God; rather, being a Christian is about knowing God. What we learn in Scripture and what we learn from our study of the doctrines of Scripture is foundational to our faith, for we can neither know God nor love God unless we know the Word of Almighty God who is the creator and sustainer of the universe. But not only is he the creator and sustainer of the universe, he is the creator and sustainer of our faith. He has created us for himself, and having chosen us in Christ before the foundation of the world (Ephesians 1:4) he has created within us new hearts—removing our hearts of stone and giving us moldable hearts to love him and serve him with all our hearts (Ezekiel

36:26). Herein is found the magnificent splendor of our salvation and the glory of our assurance of salvation in Christ.

The Assurance of Our Acceptance

Much of the reason that Christians lack full assurance of their salvation is because they do not possess a right understanding of the purpose of salvation. Most Christians think their salvation is first and foremost about them. When I begin premarital counseling with a couple in our church, one of the first things we talk about is the purpose of marriage. I usually astonish the couple when I explain to them that their marriage is not about them. After the initial shock, the young man and woman usually just look at me with blank stares. I then go on to explain that marriage is first and foremost about God and his kingdom (Ephesians 5:30–32). We spend some time talking about the creation ordinance to be fruitful and multiply, and, considering the possibility that the couple may not have children in the future, I explain that their marriage is intended to bring glory to God as each fulfills his and her covenant role in the relationship. I explain that they are getting married not just to live under the same roof with the same last name, but that their marriage is to reflect the relationship of Christ and his bride (5:25–29). When the couple understands that, they have a solid foundation on which to build a loving and full marriage.

When we begin to realize that salvation is not primarily about us, but about God's kingdom and his glory, only then are we able to have a right understanding of assurance, for we did not become Christians so that we can just live under the same roof as other Christians or for the mere reason to be called a "Christian." By God's grace, we have become Christians to be a part of the glorious bride of Christ, to become the holy temple of God and a royal priesthood (1 Peter 2:9). We became Christians because God accepted us into his family. We were dead, but by the power of the Holy Spirit, God the Father made us alive in Christ and accepted us (Acts 10:35). Though this is quite simple, it is confusing to many people who have been tricked into thinking that they have somehow accepted God. However, the Word of God is clear, it is not that we have accepted God; rather, he has accepted us. The apostle Paul writes in Ephesians:

> Blessed be the God and Father of our Lord Jesus Christ, who has blessed us with every spiritual blessing in the heavenly places in Christ, just as He chose us in Him before the foundation of the world, that we should be holy and without blame before Him in love, having predestined us to adoption as sons by Jesus Christ to Himself, according to the good pleasure of His will, to the praise of the glory of His grace, by which He made us accepted in the Beloved. (Ephesians 1:3–6 NKJV)

Paul writes that God "made us accepted in the Beloved." It is God who accepts us, not we who accept God (Psalm 19:14; Jeremiah 14:10; Ezekiel 20:40; Romans 14:3; 1 Timothy 2:3; Hebrews 12:28; 1 Peter 2:5), and if it is God who accepts us, it is God who keeps us. Jesus Christ is our Great Shepherd, and we are his sheep who hear his voice, who follow him, and for whom he laid down his life for the express purpose that we would be accepted by the Father only as a result of the Son's perfect and completely acceptable life and death (John 10:1–11).

A few years ago, the International Dairy Foods Association celebrated the tenth anniversary of its "Got milk?" advertising campaign. During the course of this campaign, just about everyone from Michael Jordan to the Cookie Monster has been featured wearing a milk mustache. And the cultural influence of these advertisements is widespread, spawning similar slogans just about everywhere: "Got termites?" "Got hair?" "Got brains?" While these are generally quite harmless, one such slogan—usually seen on a bumper sticker—is not so harmless: "Got Jesus?"

The question "Got Jesus?" presumes a number of things. Fundamentally, it presumes that one should *get* Jesus—and with this presumption I am in complete agreement. My contention, however, is with the question itself. The simple question "Got Jesus?" begs the more appropriate question: "Does Jesus got you?" Although it is not nearly as trendy, and while I cannot imagine that such a question would ever make it onto a bumper sticker, the truth of the matter is that the former question tends to distort the gospel while the latter question is at the very heart of the gospel. The notion that it is incumbent upon us to accept God, or get Jesus, is at the very heart of the problem for many Christians—they actually think that they accepted God, and therefore it is only natural for them to think that they need to keep accepting God every hour of every day in order to make it as a Christian. In his timely work *The Gospel according to Jesus*, John MacArthur writes:

> It may surprise you to learn that Scripture never once exhorts sinners to "accept Christ." The familiar twentieth-century evangelistic appeal in all its variations ("make a decision for Christ"; "ask Jesus into your heart"; "try Jesus"; "accept Jesus as your personal Savior"), violates both the spirit and the terminology of the biblical summons to unbelievers.
>
> The gospel invitation is not an entreaty for sinners to allow the Savior into their lives. It is both an appeal and a command for them to repent and follow him. . . .

The great miracle of redemption is not that we accept Christ, but that he accepts us. In fact, we would never love him on our own (1 John 4:19). Salvation occurs when God changes the heart and the unbeliever turns from sin to Christ. God delivers the sinner from the domain of darkness into the kingdom of light (Col. 1:13). In the process Christ enters the heart by faith to dwell there (cf. Eph. 3:17). Thus conversion is not simply a sinner's decision for Christ; it is first the sovereign work of God in transforming the individual.[5]

Ultimately, when we come before the throne of God, we will not be asked whether we accepted him as God or whether we accepted Jesus as our personal Christ. On the contrary, if we are in Christ we will be accepted only because God the Father accepted us in Jesus Christ, for only Christ is acceptable before the Father. We are in Christ on account of the Father's imputation of Christ's righteousness to us and the imputation of our sins to Christ. In the cross of Christ, the bride of Christ has been made acceptable to God, and such acceptance is the foundation of our assurance.

The Assurance of Our Victory

Just as our justification is from God, so our sanctification is from God, but unlike our justification, which is a monergistic work, in sanctification God calls us to work together with him to mature as Christians. As Christians we can never say to God: "The reason I still sin, or the reason I am not maturing as quickly as I would like, is because you have not given me enough grace." Nevertheless, it is not as if our spiritual sustenance is solely dependent upon our own ability to muster enough faith. Insofar as salvation is a gift from God, so faith is a gift from God (Ephesians 2:8–10). And such faith is a faith that not only saves us but sustains us as well. Our faith is fixed on one who has authored our faith and who will finish our faith as well. The author of Hebrews reminds us that Jesus is the author and finisher of our faith (Hebrews 12:2). As the author of our faith, it is not as if Jesus simply begins our faith and then stands back as we take two steps forward and then three steps back, over and over again. In fact, the author of Hebrews uses an intriguing Greek word to describe Jesus as the author of our faith: *archegos*, a compound composed of *arche* and the verb *ago*. The word *arche* is familiar to us in English words such as *archeology* and *archetype*. The general meaning of the prefix is "early," "beginning," or "at the outset of." The verb *ago* is not familiar to us, but it simply means "to lead." Together, the two make up a fascinating word, especially as the author of Hebrews uses it to describe Jesus. The word *archegos* can be strictly translated as "one who leads from the beginning," "a pioneer," or "a captain."

To illustrate the significance of the word the author of Hebrews is using, it may be helpful to consider a scene from the movie *Braveheart*. In the last battle at Falkirk, the brave William Wallace stands on the front line of the Scottish army as he leads his army into battle. On the other side of the battlefield Edward I "Longshanks" sits on his horse at the very back of his troops, sending each regiment to battle with the raising of his arm. It is a magnificent scene in which William Wallace is at the forefront of his army leading them into battle.

The author of Hebrews says that Jesus is not merely one who sits back as he tells us to fight the good fight. Rather, as the Great Shepherd who calls his own sheep by name and leads them out, going before them, Jesus Christ is the captain of our souls who leads at the forefront, from the beginning, and it is he who has gained the victory for us (John 10:3–4; 1 Corinthians 15:50–58; Hebrews 2:10; 1 John 5:4). This truth is well illustrated by the second stanza of Martin Luther's great hymn *A Mighty Fortress*:

> Did we in our own strength confide
> our striving would be losing;
> were not the right man on our side,
> the man of God's own choosing;
> dost ask who that may be?
> Christ Jesus, it is he;
> Lord Sabaoth his name,
> from age to age the same,
> and he must win the battle.

Our assurance of salvation is established by Christ's having the battle, for he is the author and finisher of our faith. Therefore, as Paul writes in Romans 8:31–39, we are more than conquerors through him who loved us. And such love is demonstrated in a special way toward us who believe. John Murray comments on this passage in his classic work *Redemption Accomplished and Applied*:

> Paul is here affirming in the most emphatic way, in one of the most rhetorical conclusions of his epistles, the security of those of whom he has been speaking. The guarantee of this security is the love of God which is in Christ Jesus. And the love of God here spoken of is undoubtedly the love of God towards those who are embraced in it. . . . We see, therefore, that the security of which Paul here speaks is a security restricted to those who are the objects of the love which was exhibited on Calvary's accursed tree, and therefore the love exhibited on Calvary is itself a distinguishing love and not a love that is indiscriminately universal. It is a love that insures the eternal security of those who are its objects and

Calvary itself is that which secures for them the justifying righteousness through which eternal life reigns.[6]

Yet it is not in our own strength that we confide, for our striving would be losing. We are conquerors, not by our own means, but on account of God's sustaining grace, as Paul teaches us regarding the "Lord Jesus Christ, who will sustain you to the end, guiltless in the day of our Lord Jesus Christ. God is faithful, by whom you were called into the fellowship of his Son, Jesus Christ our Lord" (1 Corinthians 1:7–9; see also Psalm 55:22; Isaiah 59:16).

The Assurance of God's Preservation

Although we all struggle in dealing with the sinfulness of the world, it is not only the world's sinful deceptions and sinister devices that we have to worry about (Ephesians 6:12). We also are faced with the struggle of dealing with the sinfulness of those around us, even those whom we dearly love. But what is more, we are in a constant war with our own sinfulness (Hebrews 12:4). Even though we have been declared just by God, we still sin. Though we are no longer slaves to sin (Romans 6:15–23), we still struggle to honor God in all we think, in all we say, and in all we do (12:1–2, 10). And because we still sin, we struggle with overcoming our doubts and anxieties about the gracious provision of God in salvation (Matthew 28:17; Luke 24:38). Nevertheless, by redeeming us, the Lord secured us in his hand, from which we cannot be snatched and from which we ourselves cannot escape, even on days when we feel like running away (John 10:27–29).

The God of creation is the God of history; he is the God of Scripture and the God of the covenant. At creation and throughout history, the God of Scripture calls himself "Lord."

Central to the meaning of the name "Lord" is the idea of covenant. First and foremost, Almighty God is the covenant Lord whose word is true and whose promises are faithful. As the only Lord, he is our master and our guardian, who has entered into a covenant with us by his own initiative. Just as we did not first love him, but he first loved us, so we did not initiate our covenant relationship with him. The covenant he entered with us is a covenant to bless us and keep us for himself. He has secured us once for all in the eternal bond of the blood of his only begotten Son. Nevertheless, he has secured us in Christ not only for some future date when we will be with him at home in heaven, he has secured us in Christ for the here and now. Therefore, he not only has promised us eternal life, but he assures us of our eternal life each and every day. We are reminded constantly of his sustaining grace every time we are convicted of our sin, every time we repent, every time the fear of God comes upon us, and every time we are disciplined by our heavenly Father.

Though such means are not always warmly welcomed, our loving Father preserves us in such ways. It is by his kindness that we are brought to repentance (Romans 2:4; 2 Timothy 2:25). It is through Spirit-led confession that we are cleansed from all unrighteousness (1 John 1:9). Indeed, by placing godly fear within our hearts, the Lord has caused us to remember the eternal security of his everlasting covenant with us to prevent us from ever turning away from him (Jeremiah 32:40). And as the author of Hebrews explains (12:4), it is through the Father's discipline that we are reminded of his enduring love. In Psalm 86:11–13, David prayed:

> Teach me your way, O LORD,
>   that I may walk in your truth;
>   unite my heart to fear your name.

> I give thanks to you, O Lord my God, with my whole
> heart,
> and I will glorify your name forever.
> For great is your steadfast love toward me;
> you have delivered my soul from the depths of Sheol.

Commenting on this psalm, John Calvin writes:

> In the word *unite* there is a very beautiful metaphor, convey-
> ing the idea, that the heart of man is full of tumult, drawn
> asunder, and, as it were, scattered about in fragments, until
> God has gathered it to himself, and holds it together in a
> state of steadfast and persevering obedience. From this also,
> it is manifest what free will is able to do of itself. Two powers
> are ascribed to it; but David confesses that he is destitute of
> both; setting the light of the Holy Spirit in opposition to the
> blindness of his own mind; and affirming that uprightness
> of heart is entirely the gift of God.[7]

Assurance through Purification

In Hebrews 9:11–14, the author of Hebrews explains how the
superiority of Christ's sacrifice purified our consciences:

> But when Christ appeared as a high priest of the good things
> that have come, then through the greater and more perfect
> tent (not made with hands, that is, not of this creation) he
> entered once for all into the holy places, not by means of the
> blood of goats and calves but by means of his own blood,
> thus securing an eternal redemption. For if the sprinkling of
> defiled persons with the blood of goats and bulls and with
> the ashes of a heifer sanctifies for the purification of the flesh,
> how much more will the blood of Christ, who through the

eternal Spirit offered himself without blemish to God, purify our conscience from dead works to serve the living God.

By his work on the cross for us, Christ purified our consciences so that we might be delivered from dead works in order to serve the living God. In the next chapter, the author of Hebrews ties together "our hearts sprinkled clean from an evil conscience" with his call to "draw near with a true heart in full assurance of faith":

> Therefore, brothers, since we have confidence to enter the holy places by the blood of Jesus, by the new and living way that he opened for us through the curtain, that is, through his flesh, and since we have a great priest over the house of God, let us draw near with a true heart in full assurance of faith, with our hearts sprinkled clean from an evil conscience and our bodies washed with pure water. Let us hold fast the confession of our hope without wavering, for he who promised is faithful. And let us consider how to stir up one another to love and good works, not neglecting to meet together, as is the habit of some, but encouraging one another, and all the more as you see the Day drawing near. (Hebrews 10:19–25)

The Lord who promised is faithful, the author of Hebrews asserts; therefore we should hold fast to the confession of our hope without wavering, without doubting his faithfulness, for the covenant Lord, who is the guardian of our souls, has declared that we are righteous in Christ, that our consciences have been purified. And in order to demonstrate this truth, the Lord reveals his faithfulness each and every day by pricking our consciences so that we might continually mature as his beloved children in whom he delights (1 Thessalonians 5:5; 1 John 3:1). It should not surprise us to know that the Lord God Almighty does not play games with our souls. He is our Father who continually demonstrates his love for us by revealing to us our sins, enabling us to repent, and reminding us of his holiness (Isaiah 5:16), for when we realize how holy he is—and thus how holy we are not—we grow in the grace and knowledge of God our Father (Ephesians 1:17; Colossians 1:10; 2 Peter 1:8).

The Word of God does not say that the Lord disciplines all people, but only those whom he loves (Hebrews 12:5–6):

> My son, do not regard lightly the discipline of the Lord,
>   nor be weary when reproved by him.
> For the Lord disciplines the one he loves,
>   and chastises every son whom he receives.

Such discipline is a gracious provision of the Lord whereby we are assured by God of his love for us and his protection of us. Although it sounds strange to suggest that we should long for God's discipline in our lives, when we do begin to yearn for God's loving hand of discipline and, dare I say, pray for such discipline, that is when we will experience the most wonderful growth in our lives, for it is not unto us but unto him that all glory belongs—for the sake of his steadfast love and faithfulness (Psalm 115:1). By his mercy we are not damned. By his sacrifice we have been redeemed. By his grace he has set us apart. By his promise we are granted assurance. And for his glory he preserves us to the end.

2

ASSURED FROM BEGINNING TO END

Philip Graham Ryken

> Here we see the infinite love of God, that He has been pleased
> to think of us poor creatures from everlasting and make it His
> work to reconcile us to Himself. And here is the foundation
> of the sweetness and comfort of all the mercies of God to
> those who are reconciled to Him: they are the fruits of the
> eternal love of God for us.
>
> —Jeremiah Burroughs, *Gospel Reconciliation*

Before you were born—before anyone was born, for that matter—before God made the heavens and the earth, even before
the angels first praised their maker, God was planning to save
his people from their sins. We were destined to salvation long
ages before the world was ever created.[1]

The Saving Work of the Triune God

The eternal plan of salvation required the active engagement of every person of the Trinity: Father, Son, and Spirit. In the magnificent opening chapter of Ephesians, the apostle Paul praises first the Father (Ephesians 1:3–6), then the Son (1:7–12), and finally the Holy Spirit (1:13–14) for the part that each plays in salvation. Salvation is administered by the Father; he organizes and oversees the plan of salvation. Salvation is accomplished by the Son; he died on the cross for our sins and rose again to give us eternal life. Salvation is applied by the Spirit; he takes what Jesus has done and makes it our own. Or, to put all of this a different way, the salvation that was planned by the Father has been procured by the Son and is now presented by the Spirit. But whatever words we use to describe it, the point is that our salvation from sin depends on a gracious cooperation within the Godhead.

Ephesians 1:3–14 is one sentence in the original Greek—a sentence that stretches from eternity to eternity. Here the apostle lays out the whole plan of salvation, which God has been working out since forever. This salvation began in the divine mind before the beginning of time, when the triune God planned to save a people for himself. He planned to adopt us as his own sons and daughters; he planned to redeem us from our sins by sending a Savior, his own Son Jesus Christ; he planned to sanctify us, making us holy; and finally, he planned to bring us to glory.

This great plan of salvation starts with the Father, who is the origination of our salvation:

Blessed be the God and Father of our Lord Jesus Christ, who has blessed us in Christ with every spiritual blessing in the heavenly places, even as he chose us in him before the foundation of the world, that we should be holy and blameless before him. In love he predestined us for adoption through Jesus Christ, according to the purpose of his will, to the praise of his glorious grace, with which he has blessed us in the Beloved. (Ephesians 1:3–6)

The Father deliberately blesses, chooses, and predestines his people. He lovingly bestows, reveals, and lavishes his grace. This is all part of the eternal plan of the God "who works all things according to the counsel of his will" (1:11).

The salvation that originated with the Father is located in the Son. The opening verses of Ephesians focus their undistracted attention on the person and work of Jesus Christ, mentioning his person and work no fewer than a dozen times. Everything that God does (and has done and will do) for our salvation, he does *in Christ*:

In him we have redemption through his blood, the forgiveness of our trespasses, according to the riches of his grace, which he lavished upon us, in all wisdom and insight making known to us the mystery of his will, according to his purpose, which he set forth in Christ as a plan for the fullness of time, to unite all things in him, things in heaven and things on earth.

In him we have obtained an inheritance, having been predestined according to the purpose of him who works all things according to the counsel of his will, so that we who were the first to hope in Christ might be to the praise of his glory. (Ephesians 1:7–12)

These verses contain virtually the whole message of salvation, which Paul describes as "the mystery of [God's] will" (1:9). This saving message declares that all of God's best blessings come through union with Jesus Christ. We are blessed with every spiritual blessing "in Christ" (1:3). It is in covenant with Christ that we are predestined, redeemed, forgiven, adopted, reconciled, sanctified, and glorified. Christ is not only the beginning and the end of our salvation, he *is* our salvation, for in him we receive everything we need to be saved. The location of our salvation is Jesus Christ.

The salvation that originated with the Father and is located in the Son is communicated by the Holy Spirit:

> In him you also, when you heard the word of truth, the gospel of your salvation, and believed in him, were sealed with the promised Holy Spirit, who is the guarantee of our inheritance until we acquire possession of it, to the praise of his glory. (Ephesians 1:13–14)

Since God's best blessings are spiritual, we can receive them only by his Spirit. First the Holy Spirit enables us to hear the gospel of truth, which is the message of salvation. Then he changes us from the inside out, which is regeneration. With regeneration comes the gift of faith, the spiritual ability to believe in the death and resurrection of Jesus Christ. By doing this work in us, the Holy Spirit makes our salvation a present reality. He takes the salvation that the Son accomplished in the past and applies it to us in the present. It is for this reason that the Bible teaches us that we were sealed with the Holy Spirit (1:13), which in ancient times was the proof of ownership. The sealing work of the Holy Spirit proves that we really do belong to God and will continue to belong to him for all eternity. Hence the Spirit is called "the guarantee of our inheritance" (1:14), the purchase of the spiritual transaction that God has made with us and for us. The Holy Spirit is a down payment on eternity, the security of our salvation, now and forever.

The first half of Ephesians 1 thus gives a complete overview of the work of God in saving sinners. All the blessings of salvation come from God, in Christ, by the Holy Spirit. Our salvation jointly depends on the electing, predestining work of God the Father; the redeeming, atoning work of God the Son; and the sealing, guaranteeing work of God the Holy Spirit.

Before the Foundation of the World

One of the most amazing things about the threefold saving work of the triune God is that it began in eternity past. The emphasis in Ephesians 1 is not so much on the Spirit's application of salvation in the present or even on the Son's accomplishment of salvation in the past, but on the Father's administration of salvation before the beginning of time. Our salvation was pre-destined, for we were chosen "before" the creation of the world (1:4–5). The saving work of Jesus Christ in history depends on the saving plan of God from all eternity.

It is becoming increasingly popular for theologians (including some who call themselves evangelicals) to think of God as performing without a script. They say that God is in process. Like the rest of us, he is working things out as he goes along, suffering the vicissitudes of life in this universe and changing his plans to fit the circumstances. In this view, there is a creative interchange between earth and heaven that allows human beings to influence God, even to change his mind altogether. God is not sovereign; he is a finite being who does not even know the future, but he is open to the possibilities.

This is the God of open theism, but it is not the God of the Bible. It is true, of course, that God is actively at work in human history. He blesses the righteous and curses the wicked. He answers prayers, converts sinners, and plants churches. He rules over nature and over nations. But God does all these things strictly according to the plan he established before he created the world. God's participation in history depends on his purpose in eternity. He is working everything out according to his eternal plan, a plan that predates the creation of the universe.

In one sense, all of God's plans were established in eternity. The Bible could hardly be stronger on this point than it is: God "works all things according to the counsel of his will" (1:11). What is included in God's eternal decree? Everything—everything God has ever done and everything he will ever do. In this verse three different Greek words are used to describe God's plan: *thelema* simply refers to God's will in general; *prothesis* means God's purpose, especially his foreordained purpose; and *boule* refers to God's deliberate counsel. Taken together, these words show that nothing lies outside the divine intention. God does whatever he does according to his predetermined plan.

If God works out *everything* according to his eternal decree, then his eternal decree must include the plan of salvation. This is specifically what is meant by predestination ("in love he predestined us"; 1:4–5). Predestination is one special part of God's cosmic plan. It is his sovereign decision, made in eternity past, regarding the final destiny of individual sinners.

One obvious implication of predestination is that God's grace is God's choice, which is what the Bible means by election. Election is God's choice to save particular sinners, selecting them to receive every spiritual blessing in Christ. A fuller definition is contained in the Westminster Confession of Faith: "Those of mankind that are predestinated unto life, God, before the foundation of the world was laid, according to his eternal and immutable purpose, and the secret counsel and good pleasure of his will, hath chosen in Christ, unto everlasting glory, out of his mere free grace and love" (3.5).

We ourselves could never be the origin of our own salvation. We cannot be saved by anything we do, because we are sinners who are unable and unwilling to come to God in faith. Therefore, if we are to be saved, God will have to do the saving. This does not depend on some sudden decision, but upon God's eternal decree. When we make the choice to come to God, it is only because he has already done the choosing.

Divine election proves beyond all question or doubt that salvation is by grace alone. Salvation cannot depend on anything we do because we were predestined to it before we ever did anything, even before we existed. The salvation we possess in the present, which gives us certain hope for the future, depends on a decision God made in the eternal past.

Making Sure of our Election

The doctrine of election is a difficult doctrine. It is difficult because it shows—in a way almost nothing else can—the sovereignty of God's grace. In other words, it proves that ultimately salvation depends entirely on God and not on ourselves. Salvation is neither initiated by human choice nor appropriated by human effort; it begins and ends with the sovereign grace of God's electing will. But this inevitably shatters our pride, dashing any last hope of snatching glory for ourselves.

Since we are sinners by nature, and thus desire our own glory, it is only natural that we should resist a doctrine that so thoroughly exalts God and utterly humbles humanity. However, it is important to understand that election is a thoroughly biblical doctrine. Predestination was not invented by Calvin or Augustine or even Paul, but it was invented by God himself. Simply put, the doctrine of election is plain biblical Christianity—something the Bible seems to assume rather than to see the need to defend. It is not a philosophical speculation, but a biblical revelation. Indeed, it could not be anything except a revelation, since it deals with the mind of God in eternity. Ephesians 1 teaches us something we could not otherwise know. It gives us privileged information about God's eternal counsel, divulging the divine secret that he has been planning forever to save us.

Nevertheless, even though election is a biblical doctrine, it naturally causes people to wonder whether they are among the elect. Indeed, some people experience great anxiety because they fear that they are *not* among the elect. Their question becomes: How can I know if God has chosen me? If God's grace is God's choice, and if God made that choice before I was born—in fact, even before he made the world—then how can I know for sure that I will be saved? These are reasonable questions. If salvation depends on election, then it would seem that being sure of salvation requires being sure of election.

This question is made all the more urgent because not everyone will be saved. Theologians sometimes speak of "double predestination," which means that according to God's decree, some sinners will never repent and thus finally will be lost in their sins. Strictly speaking, double predestination is not a biblical term, for the Bible nowhere speaks of anyone being predestined to hell. It reserves the verb "predestine" (*proorizo*) for the salvation of sinners unto eternal life. However, even if it is not a biblical term, double predestination expresses a biblical truth. If God has made an advance decision about which people he will save from their sins, he has also made an advance decision about which people he will leave in their sins (Romans 1:28). The theological term for this is "reprobation." It means that when God established his plan of salvation, he decided to pass some sinners by. In the words of the apostle Peter: "They stumble because they disobey the word, as they were destined to do" (1 Peter 2:8; see also Jude 4). The apostle Paul describes the reprobate as "vessels of [God's] wrath" (Romans 9:22; see also Ephesians 2:3). This prospect is so terrifying that it is little wonder the Bible should command us to make our "calling and election sure" (2 Peter 1:10). In other words, Christians are commanded to seek assurance of their election.

So how can you be sure that you are among God's elect? Here it helps to remember that the elect are chosen in Christ. Election in Christ is the only kind of election there is. What God has chosen to do is to unite us to Christ, putting us together with him for our salvation. Therefore, to ask if you are among the elect is really to ask if you are in Christ. If you want to know whether God has chosen you, all you need to know is whether you are in Christ. You do not need to read God's mind. You do not need to climb up to heaven and peek into the Book of Life. All you need is to know Jesus Christ, who is the location of salvation. Every spiritual blessing that God has to offer may be found in him, including election. If you are in Christ, you are among the elect, for the elect are chosen in Christ. John Calvin thus warns in his famous *Institutes of the Christian Religion* that "if we have been chosen in him [Christ], we shall not find assurance of our election in ourselves"; rather, Christ "is the mirror wherein we must, and without self-deception may, contemplate our own election."[2] The way to make your calling and election sure is to be sure that you are joined to Jesus Christ by faith.

Since election is in Christ, it is often best understood after one becomes a Christian. In fact, the doctrine of election is sometimes referred to as a "family secret" (although it is not really a secret to anyone who knows the Bible). While you are still outside God's family, you may not hear about predestination at all; if you do, it hardly seems to make any sense. Once you are in the family, however, it makes the most perfect sense in the world. Indeed, it is what helps to make sense of everything else.

The famous American Bible teacher Donald Grey Barnhouse often used an illustration to help people make sense of election. He asked them to imagine a cross like the cross on which Jesus died, only so large that it had a door in it. Over the door were these words: "Whosoever will may come" (see Revelation 22:17). These words represent the free and universal offer of the gospel. By God's grace, the message of salvation is for everyone. Every man, woman, and child who will come to the cross is invited to believe in Jesus Christ and enter eternal life. On the other side of the door a happy surprise awaits the one who believes and enters. From the inside, anyone glancing back can see these words written above the door: "Chosen in Christ before the foundation of the world" (see Ephesians 1:4). Election is best understood in hindsight, for it is only after coming to Christ that one can know for sure whether one has been chosen in Christ. Those who make a decision for Christ find that God made a decision for them in eternity past. It is like the words of the anonymous nineteenth-century hymn:

> I sought the Lord, and afterward I knew
>> he moved my soul to seek him, seeking me;
> it was not I that found, O Savior true;
>> no, I was found of thee.

Salvation does not come from the sinner's own choice, but from God's sovereign choosing.

The Seal of the Spirit

The personal guarantee that we have eternal life is the seal of God's Spirit, which we receive when we believe in Jesus Christ. The Scripture says: "In him you also, when you heard the word of truth, the gospel of your salvation, and believed in him, were sealed with the promised Holy Spirit" (Ephesians 1:13). There was a time when we *were not* included, when we did not know Christ. But then we came to know Jesus in a saving way, and thus we were included in Christ.

Everyone who is included in Christ in this way is marked with the seal of salvation, the Holy Spirit, who is God's down payment on eternity. By the presence of his Spirit, God brings Christ to us here and now, so that we have a living experience of his divine presence. If we know Jesus Christ in a saving way, then God is working in us to secure our salvation. This work is too important to entrust to anyone else, so God comes and does it himself. The indwelling Holy Spirit is the seal of God in the soul of every Christian.

This means that our ongoing salvation does not depend on us; rather, it depends on God's work in us. This is important because feelings tend to fluctuate. Sometimes we feel more spiritual, but sometimes we do not feel very spiritual at all. In fact, sometimes we wonder whether we even belong to Christ. If our salvation depended on us, then we would be about as stable as the stock market. But our salvation depends on God's Spirit, who is the seal of our salvation. The Spirit makes our salvation secure, like the seal on the back of a letter. Calvin writes in his commentary on Ephesians: "The true conviction which believers have of the Word of God, of their own salvation, and of all religion, does not spring from the feeling of the flesh, or from human and philosophical arguments, but from the sealing of

47

the Spirit, who makes their consciences more certain."[3] It is only natural for us to have doubts about our salvation. But if that is the case, what we need is the supernatural work of God's Holy Spirit.

In the ancient world seals were used to mark official documents, the same way they are used today on charters and diplomas. A legal paper would be drawn up, sealed with wax, and then impressed with some official insignia, like on a ring. One document that would have been sealed like this was a last will and testament, which perhaps explains why the apostle Paul goes on to describe the Holy Spirit as "the guarantee of our inheritance until we acquire possession of it" (1:14).

A deposit, of course, is a kind of promise or pledge. When someone puts down a deposit, as on a house, they are promising in good faith that they will pay the full asking price at some later date. They are not paying the whole amount right away, but they put down a deposit to show that they are serious about making the purchase.

To put this in spiritual terms, when God sends us his Spirit, he is making a down payment on eternity. The Holy Spirit is God's way of promising us that more is on the way. One day he will give us the rest of what we have coming to us: all the blessings of salvation. God will raise us from the dead. He will take us to heaven and give us the full joy of being with him forever. The Spirit's present work in our lives is a sign of our full and future salvation. Whatever experience we have of the Holy Spirit—however incomplete it may be—is a promise of eternal life. The Bible says: "He who has prepared us for this very thing is God, who has given us the Spirit as a guarantee" (2 Corinthians 5:5; see also 1:22).

A deposit is actually part of the payment—the first installment. When someone makes a deposit, they are not just promising to pay later; they are starting to pay right away. They are paying part of the purchase price in advance, thereby offering a security for the full payment.

When God gives us his Spirit, therefore, he is doing something more than simply promising to do something for us later. Since he is a deposit, the Holy Spirit is actually part of our inheritance, the first installment of eternal life. Usually an heir has to wait until somebody dies to get his inheritance, but as Christians, we enjoy ours right away. The greatest blessing is to know God, and the Holy Spirit is making that happen right now: he is giving us a personal relationship with God! It is as if he brings heaven right inside us. Heaven is where God is, and if we have the Holy Spirit, then God is with us wherever we go.

As the seal of salvation, the Holy Spirit guarantees our inheritance, backing it with the full faith and credit of Almighty God. He also proves to us that we belong to God. This idea comes near the end of Ephesians 1:14, where Paul talks about the redemption of those who are "God's own possession" (NASB). In addition to being used to make a document secure and to mark it as authentic, seals were also used in the ancient world to prove ownership. When someone put a seal on something, he or she was indicating that whatever was marked was his or her own personal property. Seals were used to show that something was someone's possession. The Holy Spirit does the same thing for every believer in Jesus Christ. He is the seal that marks us as God's possession. If we have the Holy Spirit, it proves that we belong to God.

When the apostle Paul calls us "God's own possession," he is alluding to the Old Testament, where this phrase often occurs. Moses said to the children of Israel: "The LORD your God has chosen you out of all the peoples on the face of the earth to be his people, his treasured possession" (Deuteronomy 7:6 NIV; see also Exodus 19:5; Malachi 3:17). So here is an amazing truth: we are God's treasured inheritance. It is not just that he is our treasure; it is also that we are his treasure! And it is not just that he is our inheritance; it is also that we are his inheritance! What a remarkable statement of God's love and grace!

The Holy Spirit is the seal of our authenticity, the unmistakable sign that we belong to God. If the Holy Spirit is at work in our lives, if he is convicting us of sin, if he is giving us faith in Jesus Christ, if he is persuading us that the Bible is God's Word, if he is enabling us to call God Father, if he is making us fruitful in ministry, if he is helping us grow in grace—if the Spirit is doing any of these things at all—then no matter how much we are struggling in the Christian life, we have God's seal of our eternal salvation. The Bible says: "It is God who establishes us with you in Christ, and has anointed us, and who has also put his seal on us and given us his Spirit in our hearts as a guarantee" (2 Corinthians 1:21–22). The Holy Spirit assures us that the salvation that God began in our election will be ours to the very end.

Chosen for God's Glory

This is all for the glory of God! The reason that God made us in the first place was to glorify him forever. God will see to it that ultimately he gets the glory he deserves. Since he is glorified whenever he does for us anything we cannot do for ourselves, one of the primary ways he glorifies himself is through the salvation of sinners. We are saved for God's glory, and the glory of salvation begins with God's electing grace.

In reading Ephesians 1 it is almost impossible not to be affected by its mood of joyful exuberance. This passage contains some of the most complex theological concepts in the entire

Bible, yet the apostle Paul is not merely teaching; he is at the same time praising God for the glory of his grace. The long sentence in Ephesians 1:3–14 is punctuated with praise: "Blessed be the God and Father of our Lord Jesus Christ . . . even as he chose us in him. . . . In love he predestined us . . . to the praise of his glorious grace. . . . In him we have obtained an inheritance . . . so that we . . . might be to the praise of his glory. . . . You . . . were sealed with the promised Holy Spirit . . . to the praise of his glory."

This torrent of praise contains equal parts theology and doxology. The apostle wants us to do something more than believe the doctrine of predestination; he also wants us to experience the joy that its certainty brings to Christian life and worship. Whether we speak of the origination of election with the Father, the location of election in the Son, or the presentation of election by the Spirit, it is all to the glory of God. If predestination is all to the glory of God, then to doubt his electing grace—or even worse, to deny it—is to rob God of his glory. The only way to give God the glory he deserves is to praise him for saving us from sin by his predestinating grace and to rest secure in his eternal election to the very end.

3

GUARDED THROUGH FAITH

R. Albert Mohler Jr.

Assurance after all is no more than a full-grown faith; a masculine faith that grasps Christ's promise with both hands—a faith that argues like the good centurion, if the Lord "speak the word only," I am healed. Wherefore then should I doubt? (Matt. 8:8).

—J. C. Ryle, *Holiness*

In every generation, Christians have struggled with the question of assurance in salvation. As always, the church confronts this issue as both a pressing theological question and as an urgent pastoral matter. Answering these questions anew, we are reminded once again that all doctrine is practical and that the great biblical truths of the Christian faith are meant not only for our intellectual acceptance but for our spiritual health as well.

Many Christians suffer from an absence of Christian assurance. They lack confidence in their salvation and are troubled by nagging doubts, perplexing questions, and lack of clarity about whether assurance of salvation is actually possible. At the same time, the church has always been confronted with the reality of false professions and with a pattern of apostasy that troubles the soul and raises unavoidable theological questions. How do we explain that some who profess Christ later fall away? Some even deny the faith and repudiate the gospel. Surely this must be an urgent Christian concern.

Clearly, now is the time for clarification and for the recovery of the biblical concept of assurance. Beyond the immediate questions of assurance and false professions, the church must also confront superficial and inadequate understandings of assurance—concepts often described in terms of the "security of the believer" or "once saved, always saved."

We can be sure of this: recovery of the biblical doctrine of assurance will leave Christians no less secure than proponents of security would claim, but in fact even more secure, since they are anchored by the faithfulness of Christ and by the gift of perseverance, which Christ alone works in the human heart.

The Gift of Assurance

The apostle Paul assured the Christians in Philippi of his absolute confidence "that he who began a good work in you will bring it to completion at the day of Jesus Christ" (Philippians 1:6). The logic of that passage is of vital importance. Paul's confidence was *not* that the Philippians would be able to preserve themselves. To the contrary, his confidence was in Christ and in the promise that Christ would complete the work he has surely begun in them. Similarly, Paul instructed the church at Corinth that God has given Christians the Holy Spirit as a guarantee of his promises (2 Corinthians 5:5). Armed with this knowledge, the Corinthians were urged to be of good courage and to walk by faith and not by sight. Clearly, the apostle intended believers to rest in the assurance of their salvation and to trust the promises of God, even as they saw these promises being fulfilled in their day-by-day discipleship. Coming to the end of his own life, Paul expressed personal confidence that the Lord would "bring me safely into his heavenly kingdom" (2 Timothy 4:18). His desire was that fellow believers experience this same confidence and assurance.

The same idea is present throughout the New Testament. The author of Hebrews, for example, instructed believers to "draw near with a true heart in full assurance of faith" (10:22). At the same time, this promise was combined with the exhortation that believers must "hold fast the confession of our hope without wavering, for he who promised is faithful" (10:23).

Jesus taught his disciples a great deal about assurance, ultimately establishing the believer's confidence in the Father's promises to the Son. In the Gospel of John, Jesus teaches: "This is the will of him who sent me, that I should lose nothing of all that he has given me, but raise it up on the last day" (6:39). This is a magnificent promise, and it is one that makes sense only in light of Jesus's straightforward revelation concerning the Father's sovereignty in salvation: "All that the Father gives me will come to me, and whoever comes to me I will never cast out" (6:37). Those who are in Christ's hands will never be lost, for they have been called, drawn, and given to him by the Father himself. Jesus the Good Shepherd said in John 10: "My sheep hear my voice, and I know them, and they follow me. I give them eternal life, and they will never perish, and no one will snatch them out of my hand. My Father, who has given them to me, is greater than all, and no one is able to snatch them out of the Father's hand" (10:27–29).

Thus, a consistent biblical theme emerges from the biblical text. Jesus assured his disciples that their salvation was rooted in the eternal purposes of God and that those who truly come to faith in him are safe within the mercy of God. No one is able to snatch believers out of the Father's hand, and all those who come to the Son are preserved by the Father.

Christians should find comfort in the biblical promises of assurance. This is because they are founded ultimately in the eternal purposes of God, in the Son's accomplished work, and in the Father's vindication of the Son. Those who truly come to Christ by faith are guarded, preserved, and kept by the power of God. Our Lord did not intend his people to be trapped in a constant pattern of doubt and insecurity. To the contrary, Christ instructed his sheep to trust in him and his promises. This message was affirmed by the apostles and is expanded throughout the comprehensive unity of the New Testament. Thus, the doctrine of assurance looks into eternity past to the eternal purposes of God, looks in history to the accomplished work of Christ, and looks to the future toward the perfect fulfillment of God's purpose to redeem a people through his Son.

Assurance of salvation is indeed possible and is in one sense a Christian responsibility. Pernicious doubt concerning salvation may be an indication that the believer does not truly trust the character, power, and purposes of God. Therefore, a believer's insecurity—sometimes disguised as artificial humility—can be evidence of a heart that does not adequately trust in the promises of God. This point must be strongly emphasized. Christians who are constantly or recurrently anxious about their salvation demonstrate inadequate faith in God's promises or deficient understanding of the gospel.

Our assurance of salvation has long been affirmed by those who have loved and prized the gospel. The Westminster Confession of Faith affirms that those who "truly believe in the Lord Jesus, and love him in sincerity, endeavoring to walk in all good conscience before him, may in this life be certainly assured that they are in a state of grace, and may rejoice in the hope of the glory of God, which hope shall never make them ashamed" (18.1). Nor is this assurance merely "a bare conjectural and probable persuasion, grounded upon a fallible hope" (18.2). To the contrary, it is "an infallible assurance of faith, founded upon the divine truth of the promises of salvation, the inward evidence of those graces unto which these promises are made, the testimony of the Spirit of adoption witnessing with our spirits that we are the children God: which Spirit is the earnest of our inheritance, whereby we are sealed to the day of redemption" (18.2).

Similarly, the first question of the Heidelberg Catechism (1563) asks: "What is your only comfort in life and death?" The answer is that the believer belongs to Jesus Christ, who "preserves me [in such a way] that without the will of my Father in heaven not a hair can fall from my head." Indeed, "by his Holy Spirit, he also assures me of eternal life, and makes me heartily willing and ready henceforth to live unto him." In the same way, the First London Confession of the Baptists (1646) speaks of the assurance believers may have in God's saving purposes: "Though many storms and floods arise, and beat against them, yet they shall never be able to take them off that foundation and rock, which by faith they are fastened upon."

The Southern Baptist Theological Seminary's Abstract of Principles expresses a similar confidence: "Those whom God hath accepted in the Beloved, and sanctified by his Spirit, will never totally nor finally fall away from the state of grace, but shall certainly persevere to the end; and though they may fall through neglect and temptation, into sin, whereby they grieve the Spirit, impair their graces and comforts, bring reproach on the Church, and temporal judgments on themselves, yet they shall be renewed again unto repentance, and be kept by the power of God through faith unto salvation."

New believers in Christ may find that assurance of salvation does not immediately come, but takes time as the new Christian is instructed in the faith, formed by the Word of God, and encouraged in discipleship in the company of fellow believers. Nevertheless, the Christian is to move toward maturity and a deeper understanding of God's promises and purposes in salvation.

Assurance was a major theme of the Reformers. Lecturing on Genesis 22:16, Martin Luther reminded Christians that Paul's exhortations to have full assurance meant that believers are to possess "a firm and unshakable knowledge of God's will toward us, which gives assurance to our consciences and fortifies them against all uncertainty and mistrust."[1] God never lies, Luther reminded his congregation. Thus, believers who perversely doubt their salvation impugn the character of God and insult the character of God and the accomplished work of Christ.

John Calvin directed Christians to find confidence in God's determination to save sinners: "There is no better assurance of salvation to be found anywhere than can be gained from the decree of God."[2] Calvin also exhorted believers to find assurance in the Word of God. "It is the word of God alone which can first and effectually cheer the heart of the sinner," Calvin advised. "There is no sure or solid peace to be enjoyed in the world except in the way of reposing upon the promises of God."[3]

The Urgency of Biblical Warnings

In 2 Peter believers are instructed to supplement their faith with biblical virtues and the qualities of authentic discipleship: "For if these qualities are yours and are increasing, they keep you from being ineffective or unfruitful in the knowledge of our Lord Jesus Christ. For whoever lacks these qualities is so nearsighted that he is blind, having forgotten that he was cleansed from his former sins" (1:8–9). In other words, believers are to observe their own lives, looking for the evidence of authentic faith and the marks of true discipleship. Peter summarizes his exhortation with these unforgettable words: "Therefore, brothers, be all the more diligent to make your calling and election sure, for if you practice these qualities you will never fall" (1:10).

How are believers to make their calling and election sure? There can be no question that Peter expected Christians to look and strive for the characteristics that should mark those who have been transformed by the power of God. Thus, the believer's calling and election—the very foundation of the salvation experience—would be evident in a new heart and a transformed life.

Paul also repeatedly warned Christians not to abandon their faith or to fall prey to false teachers. He even went so far as to identify some who had "nullif[ied] the grace of God" (Galatians 2:21) and others who had fallen away and abandoned their faith. Demas, for example, because he was "in love with this present world," had deserted Paul and the gospel (2 Timothy 4:10). Hymenaeus and Alexander also had "made shipwreck of their faith" and thus had been "handed over to Satan [by Paul] that they may learn not to blaspheme" (1 Timothy 1:19–20).

In pondering biblical warnings like these, most Christians think of the passages in Hebrews that have spawned so many different interpretations. How are we to understand these warnings in Hebrews, particularly 6:4–8? No doubt this is a crucial question, for how we interpret this passage is inextricably tied to larger theological issues—including the doctrine of the church itself. We should not be surprised to see that different understandings of the gospel lead to very different understandings of these passages.

Tom Schreiner suggests no fewer than six different understandings of the warnings in Hebrews 6.[4] Some suggest that these warnings reflect a possible *loss of salvation*. This position is most often associated with John Wesley and Arminianism. Wesley held that the believer could forfeit his or her salvation. More recently, Howard Marshall argues along similar lines.[5] Those who stand in the Arminian tradition suggest that believers who have genuinely come to know the Lord Jesus Christ can repudiate him and thus lose their salvation. Marshall acknowledges that this will characterize very few believers. Most will persevere to the end, and only a few will be lost. However, even with this caveat, the argument that these warnings are addressed to believers who may actually lose their salvation improperly focuses on the believer for the security of salvation, rather than on the Savior. This undermines the believer's assurance and contradicts the biblical passages that promise assurance as a gift of faith.

Second, Schreiner identifies a *loss of rewards* view, associated with figures such as R. T. Kendall and Zane Hodges.[6] Those who propose this interpretation argue for what is characteristically described as the "security of the believer." According to this view, the warnings are not about salvation at all, but they are about earthly and heavenly blessings promised to believers as rewards for faithfulness. Salvation is not in jeopardy, they hold, but believers may forfeit certain privileges and rewards by their disobedience. Believers who fail to demonstrate the signs and characteristics of authentic discipleship are nonetheless held to be secure simply because at some point in their lives they exercised an intellectual assent to the facts concerning Jesus and his work. Taken to the extreme, this view holds that even those who repudiate Christ and abandon the faith will be saved. Such easy-believism naturally translates into a misconception of assurance. How can such a position be reconciled with Scripture? There is no biblical foundation for the claim that those who finally repudiate the faith are among the saved. To the contrary, believers are warned and instructed to *continue* in the faith. Paul exhorted the Colossians that they, having been reconciled to God in the body of Christ's death, would one day be presented "holy and blameless and above reproach before him" (1:22). But he then quickly added: "*If* indeed you continue in the faith, stable and steadfast, not shifting from the hope of the gospel that you heard" (1:23).

The third view is a *test of genuineness*. Most commonly associated with the Reformed tradition, this view suggests that the warnings are addressed to the church for spiritual edification, yet those who abandon the faith are not, and never were, true believers. Proponents of this view—including leading figures of the Reformed tradition such as John Calvin, Martin Luther, and John Owen—urge believers to see these warnings as teaching that the true identity of the redeemed will be evident in that true believers persevere to the end. Those who are described as falling away in these verses are those who falsely confessed faith in Christ.

A *hypothetical* view of the warnings proposes that these verses describe a falling away that, though hypothetically possible, never actually happens. This is a tempting interpretation because it allows the interpreter to accept the verses as addressed to all Christians and yet to affirm that true Christians never fall away. Yet, it hardly seems right to suggest that the Bible is warning Christians about a hypothetical falling away that could never actually happen. If so, this would represent a significant departure from the Bible's normal mode of admonition, and there is no exegetical basis for this interpretation.

The *irresolvable tension* view proposes that the biblical promises of assurance and the warnings against forfeiting salvation are to be held in an irresolvable paradox. This view fails the test of an adequate hermeneutic (method of interpretation), since Scripture surely does not leave us torn between two seemingly irreconcilable teachings. There is indeed tension in these biblical passages, but that tension is surely resolvable.

Finally, Schreiner proposes a *means of salvation* view. According to this view, the warnings are indeed addressed to true believers, but they function as a means of grace through which those believers are preserved by the power of God. In other words, these very verses are used to mold and instruct the hearts of believers so that they will not *actually* commit the very sins against which the passage warns. There is something unmistakably attractive about this proposal. Nevertheless, it is not the most adequate interpretation of these challenging texts. In truth, *all* Scripture is a means of salvation in this sense. No verse in the Bible is not a means of grace for the believer. Why should certain difficult-to-understand passages be singled out as a means of salvation in this sense?

In reality, all of these views are inadequate. Nevertheless, the Reformed consensus concerning these passages—the test of genuineness view—is the interpretation best sustained by the biblical text. Interpreting Scripture with Scripture, we cannot assert that those who genuinely believe in Christ will actually fall away. The Westminster Confession of Faith is undoubtedly right in asserting that hypocrites and unregenerate persons "may vainly deceive themselves with false hopes and carnal presumptions" (18.1). The Bible consistently affirms that all true believers will persevere to the end.

The warnings of Hebrews 6 are seen in clearer light when put alongside Jesus's parable of the sower and the soils as found in Matthew 13 and Luke 8. Comparing the human heart to soils of the field, Jesus pointed to the reality that the church would encounter those who would "believe for a while" but would fall away under testing or persecution. When Jesus identified the shallow soil, he was certainly speaking of those whose faith would be, as described by the Puritans, a *temporary* faith. As with the soil that bore fruit for a time but withered, so with those "who have tasted the heavenly gift" (Hebrews 6:4) but fall away. Theirs was not a genuine and enduring faith, but a fickle and false one.

The person described in Hebrews as having "once been enlightened" and having "tasted the heavenly gift" (6:4) must be the one whose heart is compared to the rocky soil in Jesus's parable. This is "one who hears the word and immediately receives it with joy, yet he has no root in himself, but endures for a while, and when tribulation or persecution arises on account of the word, immediately he falls away" (Matthew 13:21). The thorny soil also falls under this same judgment, and it is very likely that this is the background for Hebrews 6:7–8: "For land that has drunk the rain that often falls on it, and produces a crop useful to those for whose sake it is cultivated, receives a blessing from God. But if it bears thorns and thistles, it is worthless and near to being cursed, and its end is to be burned."

The context and audience of the book of Hebrews also help us to understand these passages. The writer of Hebrews is concerned especially with professing Christians who were reverting to Jewish legalism. In effect, these persons were repudiating the gospel and returning to their previous beliefs and ways of life. The warnings in Hebrews are surely addressed to those who had professed Christ, had received some understanding of the gospel, and had even repented of some of their sins. They are warned of the awful consequences of falling away, but they are also revealed to have been false professors from the start. Their faith was simply not saving faith. They may have responded out of emotion, excitement, or any number of similar motivations—but they were not true believers.

The Doctrine of Perseverance and the Gift of Assurance

In the final analysis, the gift of assurance rests on the biblical doctrine of perseverance. This doctrine teaches that true believers are those who persevere in and by faith. Their endurance—having been preserved by the power of God—becomes the demonstration of their salvation and the mark of authenticity. The biblical doctrine of perseverance corrects misunderstandings implied by more superficial conceptions of the believer's state. The phrase "once saved, always saved" can mislead by suggesting that true believers may demonstrate absolutely none of the marks of gospel authenticity. These persons may never repent of their sins, may repudiate the faith, and may obstinately refuse the means of grace, and yet they claim to be saved by the Redeemer they have abandoned and repudiated. This flies in the face of Jesus's own commands concerning discipleship. True believers may fall into sin and may cause grave injury to the cause of Christ, but they cannot permanently remain in this state of rebellion.

Furthermore, the doctrine of perseverance harmoniously links the believer's assurance of salvation to the larger scheme of redemption. God's sovereignty in salvation is affirmed from beginning to end. The believer's faith in Christ, exercised as an act of the believer's will, is itself understood to be a gift of God and a result of effectual calling. Thus, the doctrine of persever- ance grounds assurance in the eternal purposes of God and in God's absolute determination to redeem his people through the cross of the Lord Jesus Christ in order to preserve Christ's church throughout all the ages. R. C. Sproul explains: "We are able to persevere only because God works within us, within our free wills. And because God is at work in us, we are certain to persevere. The decrees of God concerning election are im- mutable. They do not change, because He does not change. All whom He justifies He glorifies. None of the elect has ever been lost."[7]

In Romans 8, Paul beautifully describes our salvation as a golden chain of God's purposes and decrees. Paul reminded the Romans that it is God who justifies and protects his own. Paul linked God's foreknowledge, predestination, effectual call- ing, justification, and glorification in an unbroken sequence of God's inviolable and redemptive will. He leaves no room for equivocation or doubt concerning the matter. Believers, having already been justified, are promised that they will also be glori- fied. Thus, they are to trust in God and rest in the assurance of God's omnipotent power and saving purpose. Since God is the author of our salvation, we must trust in the promise that he will finish what he has so wonderfully begun in us. We should not be surprised that some Christians who lack understanding of this divine saving purpose or lack an adequate understanding of the gospel should be unsure of their salvation.

The promises made to the believer are secured further by the promises the Father has made to the Son. The eternal covenant of redemption is the larger context in which the doctrine of perseverance and the gift of assurance are to be understood. The

Father's will to save will be completely fulfilled in the finished work of the Son. This is the certain and unshakable ground of our confidence. Therefore, the writer of the book of Hebrews points to the completed work of Christ and to his identity as "a great priest over the house of God." Accordingly, believers are to "draw near with a true heart in full assurance of faith, with our hearts sprinkled clean from an evil conscience and our bodies washed with pure water" (10:21–22). In the very next verse, the author writes: "Let us hold fast the confession of our hope without wavering, for he who promised is faithful." That one verse summarizes the biblical doctrine of perseverance and the promise of assurance. Believers are exhorted to "hold fast the confession of our hope" but are then reminded to trust that "he who promised is faithful." Kept by the power of God, believers are preserved through faith, and genuine faith is demonstrated in the perseverance of the saints of God.

This is an important reminder for all believers. Our trust is not in ourselves, but in God who redeemed us by the blood of the Lamb and promises to guard us to the end. In this light, the biblical warnings take on a new and important significance. Those who profess faith in Christ must examine their lives, looking for evidence of the work of Christ and the substance of authentic faith. Those who claim to be Christian believers who obstinately remain in sin, who deny the faith, and who habitually absent themselves from the means of grace must see these warnings as a merciful call to repent and submit to the gospel. Nevertheless, that a believer might be troubled at heart concerning his or her salvation is almost surely an evidence of the work of God in the heart, evidence that should encourage the believer to trust in Christ. On the other hand, a perverse concern turns the believer inward and eventually focuses the mind and heart on whether to trust oneself, rather than on whether one truly trusts Christ alone.

In his first letter, Peter reminded Christians that the Father "has caused us to be born again to a living hope through the resurrection of Jesus Christ from the dead" (1 Peter 1:3). Believers are promised "an inheritance that is imperishable, undefiled, and unfading, kept in heaven for you, who by God's power are being guarded through faith for a salvation ready to be revealed in the last time" (1:4–5). The Christian's proper assurance of salvation is God's gift—a gift given to the believer by the very God who has accomplished our salvation. True believers are promised that God will guard his own through faith, even as salvation will be revealed "in the last time." In the end, the gift of assurance and the doctrine of perseverance take us back to the very essence of the gospel—we are saved by grace through faith—nothing more, nothing less.

4

ASSURED IN CHRIST

Richard D. Phillips

The facts are that the more intelligent, the deeper and the
more unwavering the assurance of salvation is, the humbler,
the more stable and the more circumspect will be the life,
walk and conduct. Where closeness of fellowship with God
is maintained, where the highest privileges of redemption
are appropriated, there holiness, love and obedience must
reign.

—John Murray, "The Assurance of Faith"

John Duncan is regarded as one of the most holy men that
Scotland produced in the nineteenth century. His vast learning
in ancient languages earned him the nickname "Rabbi," but
it was his fervent piety that earned the affection of the young
men he helped prepare for the ministry. One former student
remembered: "When we looked at 'the Rabbi' we all felt and

were wont to say, 'There is the best evidence of Christianity, and especially the best evidence that there is such a thing as living personal godliness; there is a man who walks closely with God, who actually knows what it is to enjoy the light of God's countenance."[1] Despite this, Duncan is also remembered for his lifelong struggle to gain assurance of salvation, a struggle that absorbed a considerable portion of his spiritual energy and deprived him of much joy. His experience, which typifies that of many others, prompts us to ask: What is the right foundation for assurance of salvation?

A concern in the pursuit of assurance is that we find not merely any sort of assurance but biblically warranted grounds for assurance of salvation. This was part of "Rabbi" Duncan's problem: he feared to permit himself a comforting but counterfeit assurance. This danger is illustrated by a story told by Donald Grey Barnhouse. A group of soldiers were captured during a long war and were held for years in a prisoner-of-war compound. Red Cross packages would come, and these occasionally contained Monopoly games to help the soldiers pass the time. Soldiers being soldiers, they used the Monopoly money for all kinds of transactions, but especially for gambling. Many a night was passed playing poker using the yellow, green, blue, and red pieces of money. As always happens, one of the soldiers excelled in this and succeeded at drawing most of the money into his own pockets. He became the prisoner-of-war camp's captain of industry, amassing a small fortune in his Monopoly currency. Finally, the long-awaited day came when the war ended and the prisoners were sent home. The wealthy soldier took the first opportunity to visit a bank and open an account. Proudly, he dipped into the bag he had carried from faraway and scooped yellow $100 bills and golden $500 bills onto the counter. Of course, the bank teller refused to accept any of the Monopoly money!

The point is that whatever comfort we derive from various sources that assure us of salvation, what matters most is that our assurance has currency with God. How crushing it was for the soldier to learn that he was, in fact, penniless. But how much more crushing it will be for the falsely assured sinner who spends his or her days in a spiritual comfort that in the end leads not to heaven but to hell.

Can we find a securely established assurance of salvation? In an outstanding study of this subject, John Murray shows that this is a quest limited to those convinced of Reformed theology.[2] Roman Catholics do not pursue assurance of salvation and are strongly discouraged from doing so, since for Rome justification is a process that can be sure only when it is completed. The Roman Catholic is no more secure than his or her most recent visit to the priest. The only assurance is in continued good performance.[3] The situation is little better among Arminians, who deny assurance on the grounds that salvation may be lost at any time. The Arminian insistence on a general salvation rather than a particular one—that is, a salvation that is open equally to all but effectually to none—effectively rules out assurance in this life. Murray writes: "Every brand of theology that is not grounded in the particularism which is exemplified in sovereign election and effective redemption is not hospitable to this doctrine of the assurance of faith." This is why assurance of salvation is a field of theology and Christian experience plowed only by the Reformed. Murray observes: "It is no wonder that the doctrine of assurance should have found its true expression in that theology which is conditioned by the thought of the divine atonement or effective redemption, the irreversibility of effectual calling, and the immutability of the gifts of grace."[4]

According to Reformed theology, the Bible *does* provide the believer with secure foundations for assurance of salvation. First, the believer may look with confidence to God the Father's election of particular individuals from eternity. Believers can know that they were eternally elected by God and that their eternal destiny is secure in him. Second, believers may find assurance in God the Son's effectual redemption of particular individuals for salvation and eternal life. As illustrated by the character Christian in John Bunyan's *Pilgrim's Progress*, who carried a burden of sin on his back, any quest for assurance must lead us ultimately to the cross, where Christ's efficacious redemption provides the strongest foundation for our assurance of salvation.

Redemption Accomplished

Our quest for assurance brings us, therefore, to an important theological question dealing with the nature of Christ's redeeming work. Did Christ's death effectually accomplish salvation for God's elect, or did his death merely produce a situation in which salvation is made possible? In asking this, we should first be sure of what we mean by "redemption."

Redemption is a term borrowed from the market place. Pawnshops use the word today. If one is short of cash, one may pawn an object of value by giving the pawnshop the object and receiving a certain amount of money and a receipt. If the person is able to scrape the prescribed amount of money together, he or she may bring back the receipt and redeem the object held by the pawnshop. The Bible applies this idea to the deliverance of men and women from bondage. The great Old Testament example of redemption is the exodus. The Israelites were in bondage to Pharaoh, slaves beneath his bitter yoke. It was a situation they could do nothing to get themselves out of; unless God saved them, they would remain slaves forever. But the Lord came to Moses and promised a great salvation: "I will deliver you from slavery to them, and I will redeem you with an outstretched arm and with great acts of judgment" (Exodus 6:6–7).

The New Testament takes this idea and applies it to the problem of our sin. Sin is our great problem and one that we cannot solve by ourselves. We think of sin as a small thing, indulgences that do us little harm, especially if nobody seems to be hurt. But the Bible says that the result of sin is slavery, bondage, and crushing affliction out of which we are totally unable to escape on our own. Murray therefore explains: "Redemption is directed to the bondage to which our sin has consigned us."[5] James Montgomery Boice writes: "The word redemption is used of . . . that work by which Jesus freed us from sin."[6] Paul ascribes this work to Jesus Christ in his death for us on the cross: "In him we have redemption through his blood, the forgiveness of our trespasses" (Ephesians 1:7). The Greek word for "redemption" (*apolutrosis*) is based on the root word *luo*, which has the idea of loosing or releasing something. From this verb comes the noun *lutron*, which came to signify the ransom price paid to set a slave free. Jesus's precious blood paid the penalty our sins deserved, ransoming us from God's wrathful judgment, so that we are set free from the bondage of condemnation and corruption from sin.

With this understanding, we return to the question: What was God's intended design in Christ's redeeming work? Did the cross merely provide an opportunity for all to come to Christ and be redeemed? Or did God have a more particular design at the cross—not merely making salvation possible for all but ensuring the redemption of his own people? Charles Hodge asks: "What was the design of Christ's coming into the world, and doing and suffering all He actually did and suffered? Was it merely to make the salvation of all men possible; to remove the obstacles that stood in the way of the offer of pardon and acceptance to sinners? Or, was it specially to render certain the salvation of His own people, i.e., of those given to Him by the Father?"[7] J. I. Packer ably states the Reformed position: "Calvinists define redemption as Christ's actual substitutionary endurance of the penalty of sin in the place of certain specified sinners. . . . Calvary . . . not merely made possible the salvation of those for whom Christ died; it ensured that they would be brought to faith and their salvation made actual. The cross *saves*. Where the Arminian will only say: 'I could not have gained my salvation without Calvary,' the Calvinist will say: 'Christ gained my salvation for me at Calvary.'"[8]

So bold a claim calls for biblical support. First, it is apparent from Scripture that Christ's death was an actual, rather than hypothetical, atonement for sin. Jesus bore actual sins upon the cross—not his own, but sins committed by others. Isaiah 53:12 specifies: "He bore the sins of many." Hebrews 2:14–17 says that Christ came to redeem God's children, who are also referred to as "his brothers," stating specifically that Jesus offered himself as a sacrifice "to make propitiation for the sins of the people." Hebrews 9:28 adds that Christ has "been offered once to bear the sins of many." From these and other similar passages we must conclude that Christ did not die to provide a place where we may all bring our sins; rather, in his death he bore the particular sins of many, that is, of certain actual people.

Second, it is equally clear that Christ's death made complete satisfaction for those sins that he bore. Hodge writes of Christ's blood: "It had an inherent worth which rendered it a perfect satisfaction, so that justice has no further demands. . . . No further punishment can justly be demanded for that offence."[9] This is required by Christ's divine nature and perfect holiness.

Peter writes: "You were ransomed . . . not with perishable things such as silver and gold, but with the precious blood of Christ, like that of a lamb without blemish or spot" (1 Peter 1:18–19). First John 1:7 specifically affirms this complete satisfaction for sin: "The blood of Jesus [God's] Son cleanses us from all sin."

With just these two assertions—and what Christian will deny them?—we have established Christ's atonement as an effectual redemption. He died for actual sins, and his death atoned for them completely. The question remains: For whom did Jesus make this atonement? Whom did he thus redeem? Can we apply this effectual atonement to the situation of those who will ultimately perish in their sins through unbelief? Surely not! The Bible speaks unreservedly about the condemnation of all who do not believe in Christ and the wrath of God that awaits them for their sins (Matthew 25:41–46; John 3:36; 2 Thessalonians 1:7–10; Revelation 20:11–15). If Christ's death fully paid the penalty for everyone's sins—irrespective of faith or unbelief—it is impossible that these sins could be punished again in the court of a just God. That the Bible so clearly promises God's vengeful judgment on the sins of unbelievers proves that Christ did not die for their sins.[10]

To summarize, Christ died for the actual sins of certain persons; his death was completely effectual in making satisfaction for those sins; and they are not the sins of those who do not believe. For whom, then, did Jesus die? The only answer is that Jesus died for his own people, who were chosen by God from all eternity, given to God the Son by his loving Father, and who enter into their salvation through personal faith in Christ. This being necessarily the case, it is not surprising to read so frequently of Christ dying not for people in general but for his own particular people. Paul declares his "faith in the Son of God, who loved me and gave himself *for me*" (Galatians 2:20).

He writes to the believers in Rome: "While we were still sinners, Christ died *for us*" (Romans 5:8).

If there is any one chapter that seals the Bible's teaching about Jesus's effectual particular redemption, it is John 17. How solemn it is to intrude upon our Lord's high priestly prayer, offered up on the very eve of his trial and crucifixion. Here, Jesus intimates that he entered this world with a particular work to accomplish for the Father: "I glorified you on earth, having accomplished the work that you gave me to do" (17:4). And it is clear that this work was directed toward a particular people chosen by God: "I have manifested your name to the people whom you gave me out of the world" (17:6). Jesus demonstrates how effectual is his redeeming work for them by adding to it his ministry of intercession: "I am praying for them," he confides to the Father's heart (17:9). But this ministry of intercession is only for his own particular people: "I am not praying for the world but for those whom you have given me, for they are yours" (17:9). Jesus concludes by committing his beloved disciples into the safekeeping of the Almighty Father, specifically including in their number those who will come to faith in the future through the apostles' ministry (17:20). Surely this prayer, offered at so crucial a moment in Jesus's ministry, removes any doubt that our Lord came to effect the salvation of those who belong to him and that his saving work is designed for their redemption and theirs alone.

Were it not true that Jesus came into this world—as Moses came to Egypt—actually to redeem his own particular people, believers would have no sure foundation for their assurance of salvation. Were this not true, we would join the Roman Catholic in seeking approval from the priest. Or we would labor in terror with our Arminian fellows, seeking desperately to keep ourselves in the way. To deny Christ's particular, efficacious atonement is to remove the pillar on which assurance rests. Iain Murray explains: "To deny the special love of God, and to believe that Christ loves all men equally, is to suppose that Christ has done no more for those the Father has given to him than for mankind at large. But if Christians are no more loved than those who will finally be lost, the decisive factor in salvation becomes, not God's grace and love, but something in them, and their perseverance becomes dependent upon themselves."[11] To know oneself as a recipient of Christ's special redeeming love is to have a foundation for assurance as strong as the Word of God and as potent as the precious blood of Christ.

Redemption Applied

To see that Christ's death achieved an effectual redemption does not, however, seal the matter of assurance. Instead, it leads us to another vital question: If Christ died to redeem a certain class of persons, how can I know that I belong to this blessed class? How can I know that Christ died for me in such a way that I have the comfort and joy of assurance of salvation? Here, we approach a matter in which error has done a great deal of harm to both the sincere and the insincere.

In our age of manipulative revivalism, many superficial converts find assurance in the memory of a fleeting, spiritual experience. Many have walked an aisle and prayed "the sinner's prayer." Thus assured of salvation by a numbers-obsessed evangelical culture, they assume themselves to be right before God. But without a genuine rebirth manifested in true repentance and faith, many such persons anticipate the glories of heaven in vain.

Others, many of whom are reacting against revivalism, seek assurance via the sacramental life of the church: I have been baptized, therefore I can be sure of being saved. The problem with this is that one may be baptized without being saved: no matter what school of baptism you consider, there are numerous instances of baptized persons renouncing the faith and falling away. This is why church history shows a tendency to add rituals designed to offer a superior assurance. One thinks of young Martin Luther seeking assurance by climbing the sacred stairs in Rome—supposedly the stairs that Jesus climbed on his way to Pilate's court—kneeling on each step and offering the requisite Hail Marys and Our Fathers, only to arrive at the top and ask, Did it work? This perfectly illustrates the failure of religious rites to supply a credible assurance of salvation.

In other quarters of the church, assurance is sought through evangelistic zeal by winning the requisite number of souls or by conforming oneself to the proper religious disciplines. Evangelism and spiritual discipline are generally good activities, but when it comes to assurance they leave one asking, Have I done enough?

Our earlier reflections on Christ's effectual atonement suggest another approach to assurance. If Christ died to ensure the redemption of his own, we ought to ask what Christ has done to apply redemption to his own. When we ask this question, we arrive at one clear answer: Christ, having died for his own, commissioned the Holy Spirit to apply their redemption through the gift of saving faith. Surely this is the perspective supplied by the apostle Paul in Ephesians 2:8–9: "For by grace you have been saved through faith. And this is not your own doing; it is the gift of God, not a result of works, so that no one may boast." Jesus assures us that salvation comes only to those who believe in his name (John 3:16) and also that only those who are "born of the Spirit" (3:6) are enabled to believe. "Truly, truly, I say to you," he said to Nicodemus, "unless one is born again he cannot see the kingdom of God" (3:3). The new birth is Christ's work through the Holy Spirit to enter his own into their purchased redemption, by means of saving faith. It is through faith that Jesus applies his redemption to his own, and it is through our consciousness of faith that we biblically ground assurance of salvation.

In defining faith, Murray stresses the active involvement of the believer: "It is by God's grace that a person is able to believe but faith is an activity on the part of the person and of him alone. In faith *we* receive and rest upon Christ alone for salvation."[12] This emphasis on our activity in faith is important to our discussion of assurance, because it indicates that we can and should be conscious of our own faith. And through the active exercise of our faith, believers obtain assurance of salvation.

Murray spells out the three classically defined components of saving faith. First, faith involves knowledge, assent, and trust.[13] We must know the biblical facts concerning Jesus Christ; we must believe them to be true; and on that belief we must commit ourselves to Jesus in trusting reliance. This definition reinforces the self-consciousness of faith, and from this consciousness spring the blessings of assurance. Therefore, when seeking to find grounds for assurance, we should ask questions about our faith. It is in this spirit that Paul wrote: "Examine yourselves, to see whether you are in the faith. Test yourselves" (2 Corinthians 13:5).

It is at this point that many tender souls stumble with regard to assurance. In 1871 R. L. Dabney warns us: "The habit of introspection may be abused, to divert the eyes of the soul too much from Christ."[14] Perhaps the classic example of this is the saintly Duncan, to whom I referred earlier. Here was a man with very compelling evidences for his faith. His knowledge of God's Word was vast, and he was utterly persuaded about the truth of all Scripture. As for his trust in Christ and the zeal of his commitment to Christ, his daily speech and conduct bore this out exceptionally. One biographer says: "Observe Duncan, a truly humble man, a truly loving man, to whom Jesus Christ was his delight, whose desire was to behold by faith the face of his Saviour and whose grief was to have that face hidden."[15] Yet, for all these commendations for his faith, Duncan lived in near-perpetual want of assurance and approached death with great fear because of it. It is this phenomenon that has driven many believers, including an increasing number of believers today, to recoil against any notion of self-examination and to seek assurance in external and objective means such as the sacraments or church membership. But the reality is that the Bible itself charges us to investigate the validity of our faith (Psalm 4:4; 26:2; 1 Corinthians 11:28; 2 Corinthians 13:5; Galatians 6:4). This is necessary because faith in Christ is the lone instrument of justification, so that its possession is the essential ground for assurance of salvation. Murray exhorts us: "We must not confuse morbid introspection with self-examination, and we must not think that the latter ministers to a subjectivism that is morbid."[16]

How, then, do we avoid the situation that Duncan so greatly feared (a false assurance of salvation) and the situation in which Duncan so greatly suffered (a true believer's failure to gain comfort from a rightly grounded assurance of salvation)? The answer is given, I believe, in J. C. Ryle's excellent treatment of assurance in his book *Holiness*. Ryle lists "probable causes why an assured hope is so seldom attained" and cites as his first reason "a defective view of the doctrine of justification." He then elaborates:

> I am inclined to think that justification and sanctification are insensibly confused together in the minds of many be-

lievers. They receive the gospel truth, that there must be something done *in us* as well as something done *for us*, if we are true members of Christ: and so far they are right. But then, without being aware of it, perhaps they seem to imbibe the idea that their justification is, in some degree, affected by something within themselves. They do not clearly see that Christ's work, not their own work—either in whole or in part, either directly or indirectly—is the only ground of our acceptance with God: that justification is a thing entirely without us, for which nothing whatever is needful on our part but simple faith, and that the weakest believer is as fully and completely justified as the strongest.[17]

To read Duncan's struggles with assurance is to observe the very embodiment of Ryle's warning. This eloquently presents the spiritual difficulty with which many otherwise sound believers approach the matter of their own assurance. Because of his loathing of the superficial religion that was so prevalent in his time, and also apparently because of sin tendencies early in his own Christian experience, Duncan was mortified that he might lightly grant himself assurance. Therefore, instead of examining himself for biblical signs of regeneration through the possession of simple faith, he ransacked his heart for foolproof signs of advanced holiness. For all his fervor as an evangelical preacher, for all the tenderness of his pastoral care for other tortured souls, for all his clarity of doctrine, when it came to his own peace of mind Duncan placed his sanctification before his justification, his works before his faith, and therefore sought assurance by looking for proofs of holiness in himself instead of redemption at the cross of Christ. Like many other afflicted believers, Duncan looked to himself rather than to Christ's efficacious redemption as the foundation of his salvation and assurance.

Biblical Tests of Faith

While remembering in our quest for assurance that every Christian remains in this life a redeemed sinner, is it nonetheless possible to test the validity of our profession of faith? The answer is yes. The New Testament presents clear and objective standards as to what constitutes a credible profession of saving faith in Jesus Christ, by which we may become biblically grounded in our assurance of salvation.

The apostle John presents three concise tests of our faith in his first epistle, an important aim of which is to help true believers attain to assurance. John writes: "I write these things to you who believe in the name of the Son of God that you may know that you have eternal life" (1 John 5:13). First is a doctrinal test: true believers see matters of truth in accordance with the teaching of the Bible (2:18–27; 4:1–6). He is concerned in part with heresies current in his own day, against which he asserts the need for believers to receive his apostolic testimony about Jesus: "We are from God. Whoever knows God listens to us; whoever is not from God does not listen to us. By this we know the Spirit of truth and the spirit of error" (4:6). The heresies of his day denied the deity of Jesus, so John emphasizes this doctrine: "Who is the liar but he who denies that Jesus is the Christ? This is the antichrist, he who denies the Father and the Son. No one who denies the Son has the Father. Whoever confesses the Son has the Father also" (2:22–23).

In other portions of the Bible we are informed of other doctrines we must believe, including Christ's substitutionary atonement and bodily resurrection from the dead (1 Corinthians 15:3–7) and justification through faith alone (Galatians 1:6–9). If we believe the Bible's teaching about God, Jesus, and salvation, this objectively indicates that we have saving faith. And according to Jesus's teaching, it is only by the regenerating work of the Spirit that we can "see the kingdom of God" (John 3:3). Therefore, doctrinal fidelity indicates that Christ's redeeming work has been applied to our hearts by the ministry of the Spirit.

John's second test of faith is a moral test (1 John 2:3–6; 3:4–10): "Whoever says 'I know him' but does not keep his commandments is a liar, and the truth is not in him, but whoever keeps his word, in him truly the love of God is perfected. By this we may be sure that we are in him: whoever says he abides in him ought to walk in the same way in which he walked" (2:4–6). Boice explains this: "Simply put, those who know God will increasingly lead righteous lives. It does not mean that they will be sinless. But they will be moving in a direction marked out by the righteousness of God."[18]

Ryle marks moral looseness as another cause of believers lacking assurance: "A vacillating walk, a backwardness to take a bold and decided line, a readiness to conform to the world, a hesitating witness for Christ, a lingering tone of religion, a clinching from a high standard of holiness and spiritual life, all these make up a sure receipt for bringing a blight upon the garden of your soul."[19]

Although our assurance of salvation is grounded not in our spiritual performance but only on the redeeming work of Christ, it is nonetheless God's design that a lack of godliness will result in a faltering assurance. The Westminster Confession of Faith well states that "true believers may have the assurance of their salvation divers ways shaken, diminished, and intermitted; as, by negligence in preserving of it; by falling into some special sin, which woundeth the conscience, and grieveth the Spirit" (18.4). This being the case, an incentive for continued growth in godliness is our desire for the joy of assurance that comes through increasing Christ-likeness.

The third test of faith is a social test. John mentions this repeatedly in his letter, most notably in 1 John 3:14: "We know that we have passed out of death into life, because we love the brothers." As Donald Macleod notes, faith in Christ "revolutionizes our social preference. . . . We love our fellow Christians."[20] For this reason, nurture of Christian fellowship and increased communion in the life of the church is strongly conducive to strengthening our assurance of salvation.

These tests of faith are given to inspire assurance in those with a credible faith, not to inflict doubt on those with an imperfect faith. John began: "We are writing these things so that our joy may be complete" (1:4). Assurance comes not through faith in our faith but through faith in the Redeemer Jesus Christ. We are bound to follow the apostles' teaching to examine our faith, but we must do so remembering that while our strongest faith is unable to save us, the weakest faith in Christ grasps a mighty Savior in whom we may rest our souls.

Giving Diligence to Assurance

The Westminster Confession of Faith exhorts the believer "to give all diligence to make his calling and election sure; that thereby his heart may be enlarged in peace and joy in the Holy Ghost, in love and thankfulness to God, and in strength and cheerfulness in the duties of obedience, the proper fruits of this assurance" (18.3). Our assurance is linked not only to our Christian peace and joy, but is also linked to our usefulness to the Lord. To this end, therefore, I conclude with two pieces of counsel for those seeking assurance through faith in Christ.

First, if assurance is grounded on faith, then the strengthening of faith must fortify our assurance. To this end, we should make use of the means of grace God has given: his Word, the sacraments, and prayer. Failure in this regard constitutes another of Ryle's common causes for a want of assurance: "slothfulness about growth in grace." He explains:

> Many appear to think that, once converted, they have little more to attend to, and that a state of salvation is a kind of easy chair, in which they may just sit still, lie back and be happy. . . . Such persons lose sight of the many direct injunctions to increase, to grow, to abound more and more, to add to our faith, and the like; and in this little-doing condition, this sitting-still state of mind, I never marvel that they miss assurance.[21]

This may offer one last illumination regarding the poor state of soul of saintly Duncan. Biographers point out his great intellectual brilliance and his absorbing interest in ancient languages. By his own admission, this occupied the bulk of his attention, and his intense academic habits kept him from an orderly life and from warm devotions in which his faith might have fed on Christ's redeeming work. Murray warns us against such a barren lifestyle: "Assurance is cultivated, not through special duties or counsels of perfection but through faithful and diligent use of the means of grace and devotion to the duties which devolve upon us in the family, the church, and the world."[22]

Second, since the foundation of salvation is Christ's redeeming work, let the faith from which we seek assurance always be fixed on the cross of our Lord. Let us seek assurance on the same path by which we seek to have our prayers answered, that is, in the name of the Redeemer Jesus Christ. Let us find assurance not by long meditation on our own souls, not by pondering questions of assurance itself, but through an ever-absorbing interest in the saving blood of Jesus Christ. Since his redeeming work—in its accomplishment and its application—is the foundation of our salvation, let it be the foundation of our assurance, of our joy, and of our hope. It is in this way that our quest for assurance will do the greatest good to our souls, if it keeps us often looking in faith to the cross of Jesus Christ, who loved us and gave himself for us.

5

ASSURANCE JUSTIFIED

Sinclair B. Ferguson

If you have assurance, be careful you do not lose it; keep it, for it is your life. . . . Keep assurance. First, by prayer, Ps. 36:10, "O continue thy lovingkindness." Lord, continue assurance; do not take away this privy seal from me. Secondly, keep assurance by humility. Pride estrangeth God from the soul; when you are high in assurance, be low in humility. St. Paul had assurance, and he baptizeth himself with this name, "Chief of sinners," 1 Tim. 1:15. The jewel of assurance is best kept in the cabinet of an humble heart.

—Thomas Watson, *A Body of Practical Divinity*

If, as is sometimes said, Paul's letter to the Romans represents the Himalayas of his writings, then Romans 8 is Mount Everest. Standing on its summit, Paul surveys an entire panorama of God's grace. His mind and spirit are raised in triumph. The gospel has placed him on top of the world, in a spiritual sense: "Those whom [God] called he also justified, and those whom he justified he also glorified. . . . Who shall bring any charge against God's elect? It is God who justifies. Who is to condemn? Christ Jesus is the one who died—more than that, who was raised—who is at the right hand of God, who indeed is interceding for us" (8:30, 33–34). Nothing "will be able to separate us from the love of God in Christ" (8:39).

Fundamental to this sense of exaltation is Paul's conviction that the present reality of justification guarantees its future consummation in final salvation. That, Paul says, remains true despite all opposition and in the face of the menacing powers that are hell-bent on the Christian's destruction. In the last analysis, he argues, nothing can be against us if God is for us (8:31).

However, God's being for us does not carry the simple implications we might naturally prefer. The divine logic is clear enough. Who could ever withstand God? Our problem is the way in which the divine logic expresses itself in our experience—not by removing all opposition to us but by overcoming all obstacles. Paul does not make the mistake of thinking that justification ends all opposition (on the contrary, in one sense it increases it!). Rather his point is that justification stands and lasts no matter what the opposition. To appreciate the significance of this we must explore the idea of justification a little more fully. In biblical language, to be justified is to be accounted righteous by God.

Justification—Counted Righteous

Scholars have long recognized that in Scripture the idea of righteousness is related to God's covenant with his people. God's personal righteousness is seen in there being an integrity between who he is, what he has promised to be, and what he actually does. As we relate to God, his righteousness comes to expression in either covenant blessing or covenant judgment (cursing).

Against this background, for someone to be righteous means that he or she is rightly related to God through his covenant. The righteous people in Scripture are not, therefore, morally perfect, but those who trust in the God of the covenant, seek to live in the light of it, and therefore—not least because of the provisions made for pardon, restoration, and new life in the covenant—enjoy a right standing, a right status before God.

Elijah is an interesting illustration of this. He was a "righteous" person (James 5:16). He was not perfect; but he trusted in Yahweh, and in faith his life was aligned with Yahweh's covenant word. He demonstrated that he was righteous (i.e., rightly related to God) by his confidence that God would keep his covenant threats to shut up the heavens and make them like brass and the earth like iron (Deuteronomy 28:23). Elijah's right standing before the Lord gave rise to right living in his power. The former was built on the latter. In the Old Testament, to be righteous then is to be counted in a right relationship with God by faith through his covenant, so that the life we live in an unrighteous world is an expression of this faith relationship.

Thus the Old Testament's understanding of the verb "justify" is to account someone to have a right relationship with respect to the law and thus to God himself. In the nature of the case, justification involves both a legal standing and a personal relationship. Living righteously flows from this, never the other way around. Therefore, the use of "justify" is a statement about a person's status; it is not a statement about the change of a person's inner condition and disposition. Despite the form of the word in English (from Latin *iustus* ["righteous"] and *facere* ["to make"]), in the Bible the verb "justify" means "to count righteous" not "to make righteous."

This becomes clear when we see that the antithesis of "justify" is "condemn," which also refers to a status. Deuteronomy 25:1 illustrates this: "When men have a dispute, they are to take it to court and the judges will decide the case, acquitting [justifying or declaring righteous] the innocent and condemning [declaring guilty] the guilty" (NIV). Here, clearly, a declarative sense alone is appropriate. To condemn does not involve the creation of a subjective, moral condition, but the accounting of a status (Proverbs 17:15; Luke 7:39).[1]

Perhaps the most arresting use of this language in Scripture is its use in connection with Christ's resurrection (1 Timothy 3:16). This was a divine speech-act in which God was reversing the verdict of the human court that had cried "guilty . . . crucify." The Father was saying, "righteous . . . resurrect!" He thus reversed the false verdict of humanity on his Son, our substitute.

Justification—Jesus's and Ours

There is in fact a very close connection between Christ's resurrection-justification and ours (Romans 4:25). This gives us a further clue as to how justification underpins assurance. If Christ's justification in resurrection is the basis for our justification in union with him, then our justification will share the same declarative quality. Unlike him, however, our justification does not take place simultaneously with our final resurrection. We might say that in our Lord's case, his "justification" was written all over him in his resurrection. In our case, our real and final justification is hidden from the eyes of the world; it is only partially revealed in our Christian lives. But one day it will be fully manifested in the final resurrection.

When we grasp that our justification is intimately related to that of Jesus, we come to understand something vital about its nature. His justification was once-and-for-all. Being raised from the dead he will never die again. God's verdict on Jesus will be neither reversed nor repeated. It was once and for all—final. But precisely because we are justified in him—that is, in his justification—our justification is also final and irreversible. Indeed we can be so bold as to say that we are as *fully* justified before God as our Lord Jesus is. We are as *finally* justified as our Lord Jesus is. We are as *irreversibly* justified as our Lord Jesus is. The only justification we have—our only righteousness—is that of the Lord Jesus. We are justified with his justification.

In more technical language we can say that in justification the ungodly are constituted *eschatologically* righteous. That is to say, our righteousness is a complete and final righteousness that encompasses all eternity. This evokes the confidence of Romans 8:1 that no condemnation is possible for us; not only are we pardoned, in a neutral position, but Christ's whole righteousness wrought out in his obedience to death *and* his last-day vindication in his resurrection has been counted to us. Thus, we are constituted righteous (5:19). We are justified by the redemption that is *in him* (4:24).

In Paul's teaching, the heart of the matter is located in Christ's role as the Second Man and the Last Adam (Romans 5:18–21; 1 Corinthians 15:45–49). Christ is "Adam" because he was made like us in every respect, yet without sin. He is "second" because there is none between Adam and Christ who enters the world without sin. But he is also second in the sense that he came not to the garden in which Adam was placed, but to the wasteland that Adam left behind. He is "last" because no other Adam is needed. He perfectly accomplished what Adam failed to do, and he reversed what Adam brought about as the consequence of his sin.

But what, exactly did this Second Man and Last Adam do? He became one with us in our flesh in order to provide a righteousness in and for our humanity by his perfect obedience to the law of God and by his offering himself as an atonement, life for life, substituting himself for us under the curse of God (Galatians 3:13). He both keeps the law on our behalf and pays the penalty for our breach of it. Since we are united to him (and here is the genius and importance of union with Christ), what is ours by nature became his by assumption, so that what was accomplished by him throughout the whole course of his incarnation might become ours by union. His lifelong obedience, his sacrifice, his resurrection—that is, his righteous life, his substitutionary condemnation, and then his justification—all are ours through what the Reformers called "the wonderful exchange" (*mirifica commutatio*) he makes with us.

He was pierced for transgressions that were ours. He was crushed for iniquities that were ours. He was punished to deal with "dis-peace" that was ours. He was wounded to heal the disease that was ours (Isaiah 53:5). He who knew no sin was made to be sin, so that we who know sin might be made righteous in him (2 Corinthians 5:21).

Or in covenant-specific language: Christ became a curse for sinners. We become blessed in Christ (Galatians 3:13). He "sealed my pardon with his blood"[2] by bearing our guilt and punishment. He grounds our final righteousness before God by his own perfect obedience. Consequently, justification not only deals with past guilt, but also secures for us a complete and final (or eschatological, to use the technical term) righteousness before God. This is what it means to be justified by faith.

Justification by Faith Alone

In a daring passage in his *Institutes of the Christian Religion*, John Calvin reminds us: "as long as Christ remains outside of us, and we are separated from him, all that he has suffered and done for the salvation of the human race remains useless and of no value for us."[3] Consequently we find in Scripture an invariable relationship between what Christ has done and how we actively appropriate it. Calvin says: "We obtain this by faith."[4]

The New Testament expresses this central role of faith in various ways: We are justified *through* faith (*dia pisteos*) (Romans 3:22) and *by* faith (*ek pisteos* or *pistei*) (3:28, 30–31). But justification is never said to be *on account of* faith (*dia ten pistin*). Faith is never the ground or foundation for justification. Faith is always and only the recipient (the instrumental cause, to employ the older language of Calvin and others). Thus, according to the Westminster Confession of Faith: "Faith, thus receiving and resting on Christ and his righteousness, is the alone instrument of justification" (11.2).

Paul stresses this point in Romans 4, in which he demonstrates in the case of Abraham that justification came not through works (4:1–8), or by the instrument of sacramental administration (4:9–12), or by keeping the law (4:13–15). Then, as now, justification is by way of faith. The important point is that the object of faith is always the covenant promise (in the Old Testament) or its fulfillment, Christ (in the New Testament), and not justification itself.

Why is faith the appropriate instrument in justification? At one level, the answer is that, since justification is in Christ, it can be ours only through personal fellowship with Christ. Faith involves such fellowship since it unites us to Christ. At another level, the answer is that, while faith is actively engaged in receiving Christ, it is in its nature receptive, noncontributory in relation to salvation. It has no constructive energy of its own. It is complete reliance on another. Faith is Christ-directed, not self-directed; it is Christ-reliant, not self-reliant; it involves self-abandonment, not self-congratulation.

Consequently, as Paul reasons in Romans 3:27: "Boasting . . . is excluded." He asks: "On what principle" (NIV) does this exclusion take place. His answer is thought provoking. It is not excluded by the principle of works. In fact, the principle of works leaves open the possibility of boasting, because the works principle always leaves room for human achievement, at least in theory. Rather, boasting for Paul is excluded on the principle of faith. Why? Because by definition faith excludes the possibility of boasting.

Thus Paul is able to say that "the promise [of justification] comes by faith, so that it may be by grace" (4:16 NIV). To say "by faith" implies "by grace" because of the very nature of faith, for faith draws everything from Christ, and it contributes nothing to him. Faith is simply a shorthand description for those who abandon themselves unreservedly to Christ, whom God has made our righteousness. Therefore, says Paul, "let him who boasts, boast in the Lord" (1 Corinthians 1:31).

Justification and Sanctification

Salvation, including justification, Paul argues is by faith, not by works. Yet, at least at first sight there is a paradox here, if not a problem. It involves the charge that has often been leveled against the Reformation's doctrines of *sola gratia* ("grace alone") and *sola fide* ("faith alone"). The accusation is that the justification of sinners by faith alone is a legal fiction and that faith alone leads inevitably to antinomianism.

How are we to respond to this? The groundwork we have established points us in the right direction—the direction that Reformed theology has consistently taken:

1. Justification takes place only in union with Christ and can never be abstracted from union with Christ.
2. In this union in which we are justified, Christ who becomes our righteousness also becomes our holiness or sanctification (1 Corinthians 1:30).
3. While justification and sanctification must never be confused, they never actually exist apart from each other. Both are ours in our faith-union with Christ. We believe *into* union with Christ.

While justification does not depend on sanctification, it is always coexistent with it. Both become ours immediately and simultaneously through faith in Christ. Since justification is God's last-day verdict about us, it is complete and final. It has been marvelously brought forward for us to enjoy in the present day.

On the other hand, holiness in Christ is his present-day work within us, and because it is progressive it will not be completed until the last day. The two realities belong to different dimensions; but they belong together in Christ. To imagine that we could receive justification but not be inaugurated into the process of sanctification would be to imagine that the person and work of the Savior could be divided into a series of electives from which we can choose. But, as Calvin regularly said, to divide the work of Christ for our justification and sanctification would be to "rend Christ asunder. . . . Let believers, therefore, learn to embrace Him, not only for justification, but also for sanctification, as

He has been given to us for both these purposes, that they may not rend him asunder by their own mutilated faith."[5]

True Faith

Two important passages in the New Testament can help us understand this point. The first passage is James 2. The question arises here whether the New Testament's teaching is either so consistent or so straightforward as we suggest. James appears to stress the importance of works in our salvation. Indeed he says that we are not justified "by faith alone" (2:24).

But the sharp words of James simply confirm the point we are making: true faith unites us to Christ and therefore does not exist without its fruit in good works; the justified individual is the being-sanctified individual, for James uses the idea of "faith" to describe two different professing believers, but makes clear that the faith of one does not—indeed cannot—save, for the simple reason that it is not genuine faith. Essentially, James is asking questions about the nature of saving faith. In order to understand his teaching properly, it may help to outline the two types of faith he is speaking about. Faith A is defined by James as follows:

- faith without deeds (2:14, 18, 20, 26)
- faith in contrast to deeds (2:18)
- faith in itself (i.e., unaccompanied by action) (2:17)
- faith alone (i.e., isolated from deeds) (2:24)

This faith is distinct from Faith B, which is defined as follows:

- faith shown by what it does (2:18)
- faith accompanied by actions (2:22)
- faith consummated by actions (2:23)

Can Faith A save, James asks (2:14)? The form of his question anticipates a negative answer. Why? Because Faith A does not work. But saving faith always works. Unless professed faith is working faith, it is not saving faith and therefore cannot be true faith (Galatians 5:6). Put another way, James is saying that if the person who believes is not also the person who works, then that person does not believe with a faith that is unto justification and, therefore, that person does not believe truly. The person who believes is thereby united to Christ in the power of his resurrection life, and such a person, sanctified in Christ, works for his glory. John Murray puts it this way: while faith alone justifies, "a justified person with faith alone would be a monstrosity which never exists in the kingdom of grace."[6] And Calvin teaches: "We confess with Paul that no other faith justifies 'but faith working through love.' But it does not take its power to justify from that working of love. Indeed it justifies in no other way but in that it leads us into fellowship with the righteousness of Christ."[7]

This is also what the Westminster Confession of Faith is at pains to emphasize: "Faith . . . is the alone instrument of justification; yet it is never alone in the person justified, but is ever accompanied by all other saving graces, and is no dead faith, but worketh by love" (11.2).

Dying to Sin

The second important New Testament passage pertaining to the believer's sanctification is Romans 6, in which Paul argues that the believer cannot go on sinning. Why not? It is simply because the grace that brings about faith reigns through righteousness to eternal life (5:21). To go on sinning would be to contradict the style of the reign of grace; it would be to contradict grace itself. Believers are those who have "died to sin" (6:2). It follows that, if they have died to sin, they cannot go on living in it. Moreover, they have also been raised with Christ into newness of life (6:4–5). There is a double reason why the old way of life is impossible for the justified.

True, we live "between the times" as Paul's subsequent exhortations make plain (6:12–14). To employ the illustration made famous by Oscar Cullmann and inspired by events that brought World War II to an end, while D-Day has already taken place in the cross and resurrection of Christ, V-Day is yet to arrive.[8] In the meantime, the conflict with sin continues to be real and painful. However, such conflict takes place within the context of the decisive victory having already been won; the final conquest is assured. There may still be bloodletting; but the end result is not in doubt.

Grace *reigns* through righteousness *in us* as well as *for us*. Thus, the Westminster Confession of Faith states: "Although the remaining corruption for a time may much prevail, yet, through the continual supply of strength from the sanctifying Spirit of Christ, the regenerate part doth overcome; and so the saints grow in grace, perfecting holiness in the fear of God" (13.3).

Justification is a status, sanctification a condition. They must always be distinguished from each other, but they do not exist apart from one another any more than Christ can be divided. But how do justification and sanctification relate to the assurance that the Christian enjoys?

Justification and Assurance

Assurance is the conscious confidence that we are in a right relationship with God through Christ. It is the confidence that we have been justified and accepted by God in Christ, regenerated by his Spirit, and adopted into his family and that through faith in him we will be kept for the day when our justification and adoption are consummated in the regeneration of all things.

The theology of assurance is simple and logical: justification is final. But experiencing assurance can be complex for the simple reason that we ourselves are deeply complex individuals; there may be much in our natural psyche that militates against assurance. It may take time before we who are loved know that we are truly loved, and it may take time before we who are forgiven understand and enjoy that we are indeed forgiven. Hence the Westminster Confession of Faith notes that "a true believer may wait long, and conflict with many difficulties before he be partaker of it." Nevertheless he or she "may, without extraordinary revelation, in the right use of ordinary means, attain thereunto" (18.3).

It was this conviction—if anything expressed with even greater vigor—that marked the Reformation in the sixteenth century. Indeed, in some senses, the Reformation was the great rediscovery of assurance. If the gospel was the power of God for salvation, if in Christ we are accounted righteous before the Father—so the Reformers understood—since earthly fathers lavish on their children assurances of their love, protection, and provision, how much more does our heavenly Father lavish on us his love, protection, and provision! Yet in many ways this was a dramatic reversal of both doctrine and experience within the history of Roman Catholicism. It may be helpful in this context to provide a brief overview of church history leading to the Reformation.

Medieval Lack of Assurance

The leading theologians of the Middle Ages represent a very wide variety of doctrinal and pastoral opinions. At one end of

99

the spectrum, Pope Gregory I the Great (540–604), from whose time the Middle Ages are usually dated, regarded assurance of salvation as basically impossible and even undesirable. At the other end of the spectrum, Thomas Aquinas (1225–74) was somewhat more judicious. He believed that assurance might come by various means: by special revelation or by signs of grace in an individual's life. But such special revelation was reserved for very few Christians, such as the apostle Paul, and in any case, Aquinas believed, the evidences of the marks of grace are very uncertain indeed. Assurance was possible—but only in theory. It could not be regarded as the inheritance of every Christian.

Aquinas's position was later confirmed as the orthodox position of Roman Catholicism by the Council of Trent (1545–63): "No one can know with a certainty of faith . . . that he has obtained the grace of God" (Canons and Decrees of the Council of Trent, sixth session, §9).[9] Indeed, Cardinal Robert Bellarmine (1542–1621), who was proclaimed a *Doctor Ecclesiae* in 1931, went so far as to write: "The principle heresy of Protestants is that saints may obtain to a certain assurance of their gracious and pardoned state before God" (*De justificatione* 3.2.3).

Rome seriously misunderstood the teaching of the Reformation. But, in addition, Rome's underlying double fear was that assurance would lead to a libertarian approach in personal morals and ecclesiastical authority. Nevertheless, there was still a more sinister element behind this, for, given the penance-oriented order of salvation of Roman Catholicism, assurance was inevitably and necessarily denied. Any way of salvation that depends on something that we must contribute ("doing what is in you" in the medieval theological language, or in its modern form: "heaven helps those who help themselves") can never bring assurance to us, for we can never be sure we have done enough to help.

Reformation Breakthrough

The Reformation was born out of this womb. Luther's spiritual experience, and perhaps also Calvin's, can be understood as a search for a truly gospel-centered understanding of the assurance of salvation. How can we be sure of Scripture, of Christ, of grace, of salvation? These were the great Reformation questions to which the Reformation watchwords gave reply. Scripture alone (*sola Scriptura*) is sufficient to give the certainty of our salvation that is accomplished by grace alone (*sola gratia*), through faith alone (*sola fide*), because of Christ alone (*solus Christus*) for the glory of God alone (*soli Deo gloria*).

On this central point, Reformed theology at its best and wisest has spoken with one voice: it is possible to have assurance of salvation without extraordinary revelation. The first recipients of Scripture possessed the assurance of salvation; Christians throughout the ages have possessed assurance; we may have assurance as well. Believers "may in this life be certainly assured that they are in a state of grace, and may rejoice in the hope of the glory of God" (Westminster Confession of Faith 18.1).

Pathway to Assurance

As the theologians of the Reformation studied the Scriptures, it became clear to them that the Lord gives assurance to us, his children, as we come to faith in Christ, as we gain a clear understanding of the grace of Christ, as we walk in the way of Christ, and as we experience the witness of the Spirit of Christ (Westminster Confession of Faith 18.2).

Faith in Christ

Christ is the source of salvation. Faith is the means by which we draw that salvation to ourselves. Faith is trust in Christ as the one who is able to save. There is already a kind of assurance seminally inherent in such faith. Indeed, faith in its first exercise is an assurance about Christ. The enjoyment of assurance is simply the inner nature of faith bursting out into our conscious awareness of what it means.

Grace of Christ

Faith seeks understanding (to use the idea of Augustine and Anselm). It is possible, of course, to have little knowledge and considerable assurance, but that is because faith has nourished itself richly even on relatively limited knowledge of a great Savior. Correspondingly, it is possible to have much knowledge and little assurance; that is because faith has starved itself by failing to feed on the knowledge it has.

The clearer and fuller appreciation we have of the nature of God's grace in Christ and all the spiritual blessings that are ours in him (Ephesians 1:3–14), the greater will be our enjoyment and assurance of this grace. Here three chief enemies rear their heads:

1. We smuggle our own contributions into the foundation of our salvation.
2. We find it difficult to believe that we are freely justified by the Father who in his love sent his Son for us. We forget that God the Father is absolutely, completely, and totally to us what he reveals himself to be to us in Christ (John 14:7, 9). Understand this, and faith strengthens while assurance is nourished.

3. We fail to recognize that justification is both final and complete. Justification is final because it is the final-day, irreversible, divine verdict on our lives pronounced now. Justification is complete because we are as righteous before the Father as Christ himself is, because we are righteous with his righteousness.

Way of Christ

Low levels of obedience are incompatible with high levels of assurance. If Christ is not actually saving us—producing in us the obedience of faith in our struggle against the world, the flesh, and the devil—then our confidence that he is our Savior is bound to be undermined, imperceptibly at first perhaps, but nevertheless really. This is why there is a strong link in the New Testament between faithfulness in the Christian walk and the enjoyment of assurance. Obedience strengthens faith and confirms it to us because true faith is always marked by what Paul calls "the obedience of faith" (Romans 1:5).

The Spirit's Witness

We are assured of salvation, Paul notes, because "we cry, 'Abba, Father!' The Spirit himself bears witness with our spirit that we are children of God" (Romans 8:15–16). Paul's point is essentially simple. Our conscious reflection that we are God's children, and therefore assured of his grace, is sometimes obscured by various things. But the word that issues from our hearts when we are in need and cry out to him—"Father!"—is itself an expression of a deep-down assurance that we are his. In fact Paul employs a verb (*krazo*) that is elsewhere expressive of a cry of need or pain (Mark 15:39 variant reading; Revelation 12:2). Here it is a child's appeal for help to *Abba*, Father!

Assurance, then, is not reserved only for Christians who have attained to the highest and holiest of conditions ("saints" in the Roman Catholic sense); it is for all of God's children ("saints" in the biblical sense) even—indeed, especially—at their weakest and neediest.

Of course, there are obstacles, as we have hinted. We cannot here explore them all. We are prone to confuse the foundation of salvation in grace (justification) with its fruit in our lives (sanctification); we obscure the enjoyment of our privileges by failure to take seriously our responsibilities; we are confused by our afflictions; we fail to appreciate the continuing presence of sin and are destabilized by our own failures; in some instances our natural temperament, our damaged mindset, may be a special hindrance to assurance; an attack of the devil may flood our minds with doubts and fears; our own consciences can hinder assurance by condemning us, and they need to be cleansed. This may all be true. But the seed of assurance that is present in faith will—as it is nourished by the truth of God's promise, the knowledge of his character, the grace of his Son, and the witness of his Spirit—press through even the poor soil of our hearts and grow to full assurance of salvation!

Effects of Assurance

We must briefly notice some of the fruits of assurance in our lives. In fact, rather than produce antinomianism and license (as Rome feared), assurance produces their opposite. Again, the Westminster Divines describe this succinctly and wisely. In assurance our hearts are enlarged by grace (1) in peace and joy, (2) in love and thankfulness, and (3) in strength and cheerfulness in duties (Westminster Confession of Faith 18.3).

This echoes the joyful confidence of New Testament faith whose enjoyment of assurance produced boldness in witness; eagerness and intimacy in prayer; poise in character in the face of trial, danger, and opposition; and joy in worship. It is worth asking if the lack of these things is evidence of a lack of the assurance that produces them. Rather than lead to presumption, assurance actually produces true humility, faithful obedience, joyful worship, for true Christian assurance is not self-assurance and self-confidence, but confidence in the Father, confidence in the Son, and joy in the Spirit. "Blessed assurance" indeed![10]

6

THE FULLNESS OF GRACE

Joel R. Beeke

In this present life there is no greater joy or contentment, nothing more certain or necessary for rising above all the difficulties we face, than to know and feel that we are children of God. When this foundation is laid, we can be sure that all that happens to us is in some way a blessing of the heavenly Father. It is a means, an aid, a path that in his providence he has prepared either to lead us toward eternal life or to increase our glory in it.

—Jean Taffin, *The Marks of God's Children*

Assurance of faith is the conviction that one has been redeemed by Christ and will enjoy everlasting salvation. A person who has assurance not only trusts Christ's righteousness as salvation, but also knows that he or she so trusts and is loved by God for Christ's sake. Such assurance is broad in scope. It includes freedom from the guilt of sin, joy in our relationship with the Triune God, and a sense of belonging to the family of God. In 1852 James Alexander said that assurance "carries with it the idea of fullness, such as of a tree laden with fruit, or of a vessel's sails when stretched by a favouring gale."[1]

In examining the importance of assurance, we must also view the development of the doctrine of assurance in Scripture, which provides clarification on several difficult or frequently misunderstood texts. And we must investigate whether Old Covenant believers were justified by grace alone through faith alone just as New Covenant believers are.

Importance of Assurance of Faith

Assurance has always been a vitally important subject, but it is even more so now because we live in a day of minimal assurance. The main fruits of assurance, such as desire for fellowship with God, yearning for his glory and heaven, a godly walk of obedience, and intercession for missions and revival, appear to be waning among contemporary Christians. This stems from the modern pulpit's emphasis on earthly happiness supplanting the conviction that we are pilgrims traveling through this world on our way to God and glory.

The need for a biblically based doctrine of assurance is compounded by our culture's emphasis on feeling. How we feel often takes precedence over what we know or believe. This attitude has infiltrated the church. The dramatic growth of the charismatic movement can be attributed in part to a formal, lifeless Christianity, for the movement offers adherents emotion and excitement to fill the void created by a lack of genuine assurance of faith and its fruits. We desperately need rich doctrinal thinking coupled with vibrant, sanctified living. There are five important reasons for seeking to grow in assurance.

Soundness of Faith and Assurance

Our understanding of the assurance of faith determines the soundness of our understanding of spiritual life. We can be sound in many areas but be unsound in our understanding of this key doctrine of Scripture. Many people mistakenly think they are Christians. We fear that tens of thousands who consider themselves Christians have fallen prey to what is often called "easy-believism"—that is, a superficial belief in Christ for salvation in response to a superficial conviction of sin. Such converts have little conception of the depth involved in the New Testament concept of faith (Greek *pistis*), which involves the entire surrender of the person upon the object of faith, Jesus Christ, trusting in him alone for gracious salvation, despite one's radical depravity.

Peace with God

Assurance is inseparable from the peace and comfort of the gospel. Paul speaks of the peace of God passing our understanding, removing our anxiety, and keeping our "hearts and minds through Christ Jesus" (Philippians 4:4–7 KJV). In Philippians, Paul reminds us of our calling: "That ye may be blameless and harmless, the sons of God, without rebuke, in the midst of a crooked and perverse nation, among whom ye shine as lights in the world" (2:15 KJV). Surely one way that a Christian can shine as a light in this evil world is by having an air of peace and joy. This does not mean that Christians will not have times of sorrow over sin, difficulties, and doubts. Paul spoke of being "sorrowful, yet always rejoicing" (2 Corinthians 6:10 KJV). Scripture is abundantly clear that Christians normally should exhibit peace and joy in the Lord (Nehemiah 8:10; Philippians 4:7). To do so, we must be assured of our faith.

Christian Service

An assured Christian is an active Christian. Paul said of the Thessalonians: "For our gospel came not unto you in word only, but also in power, and in the Holy Ghost, and in much assurance" (1 Thessalonians 1:5 KJV). The preaching of the gospel was blessed in Thessalonica so that there was "much assurance." Paul goes on to say: "So that ye were examples to all that believe in Macedonia and Achaia. For from you sounded out the word of the Lord not only in Macedonia and Achaia, but also in every place your faith to God-ward is spread abroad, so that we need not to speak anything" (1:7–8 KJV). How amazing! The Thessalonians, newly converted, "sounded out" the Word of God—that is, they evangelized—so that when Paul came into their area he discovered that the Word of God had beat him there. These people were so zealous for God because, for one thing, they were assured of their salvation.

A Christian without assurance is seldom concerned about good works. Rather, his or her spiritual energy is consumed by wondering if he or she is saved. J. C. Ryle states in his classic work *Holiness*: "A believer who lacks an assured hope will spend much of his time in inward searchings of heart about his own state. Like a nervous, hypochondriacal person, he will be full of his own ailments, his own doubtings and questionings, his own conflicts and corruptions. In short, he will often find that he is so taken up with his eternal welfare that he has little leisure for other things and little time for the work of God."[2]

Communion with God

Assurance is valuable because it enriches our communion with God. How can a person have close communion with God when he or she is afraid that God is always angry? How difficult it would be to have a close relationship with a child who is always afraid of us. The child never relaxes and accepts our expressions of love. In such an atmosphere, a close relationship is impossible. By contrast, consider the assurance implied in the Song of Solomon when the bride says: "My beloved is mine, and I am his" (2:16 KJV). There is communion here: fellowship, a warm and trusting relationship, love, and confidence on the part of the bride that the love is mutual. That is the kind of fellowship that the Lord wants with his people. He often describes his relationship to them in the closest of terms: father and child, bridegroom and bride, husband and wife, head and body. Assurance is necessary to be cognizant of such relationships.

Holiness to the Lord

Finally, assurance is critical because it makes a person holier. Speaking of the assurance that flows out of knowing that we are adopted children of the Father, John says: "Every man that hath this hope in him purifieth himself, even as he is pure" (1 John 3:3 KJV). Assurance that does not lead to a holier walk is false assurance. The person whose assurance is well founded, who experiences peace and joy, who is active in the Lord's service and lives in close fellowship with him, will be a holy person. A believer cannot enjoy high levels of assurance while he or she persists in low levels of holiness.

Kinds and Degrees of Assurance of Faith

All Scripture affirms that assurance is rooted in faith that trusts God's gracious redemption in Christ and his word of promise. Assurance that flows from each exercise of faith (Hebrews 11:1), applied promises (2 Corinthians 7:1), inward evidences of grace (1 John), and the witness of the Spirit (Romans 8:16) enables the believer to live the life of faith increasingly indebted to God's grace and in comfort and peace before God.

Robert Letham shows in detail that saving faith and assurance are intimately intertwined throughout Scripture.[3] Even the cursory summary of his work below, set in the flow of the progressive history of redemption, reveals that his thesis is in accord with Scripture.

Assurance in the Old Testament

Already in Genesis 15:6, in response to a sovereign, monergistic covenant of grace, Abraham responded with a firm, assured reliance that depends exclusively on the testimony of Yahweh (sometimes spelled Jehovah). Geerhardus Vos suggests that this verse might best be translated that Abraham "developed assurance in Jehovah."[4] Abraham fixed himself by faith upon his covenant God with growing assurance. That assurance enabled him to fix himself so confidently on abiding and eternal realities that he was able to leave his homeland in unconditional obedience to the call of God (Hebrews 11:8–19). The strong implication of Genesis 15:6, developed in Romans 4 and Hebrews 11, is that Abraham's faith involved assurance of his own salvation, for he was "strong in faith, giving glory to God: and being fully persuaded that, what he had promised, he was able also to perform" (Romans 4:20–21 KJV).

The concept of faith as trust or reliance on Yahweh runs throughout the entire Old Testament. Depending on the preposition used, faith can refer to trust placed *on* the person of Yahweh (Psalm 31:14; Proverbs 28:25; Jeremiah 49:11), *in* him (2 Kings 18:5; 1 Chronicles 5:20; Psalm 143:8; Proverbs 16:20; Zephaniah 3:2), or directed *to* him (2 Kings 18:22;

Psalm 86:2; Proverbs 3:5). Israel's confidence in Yahweh and his redemptive work in covenantal history is of an assuring nature. Saving faith in the Abrahamic covenant was synonymous with trusting in and relying upon Israel's faithful, covenant-keeping God, assured that his covenant promises would be fulfilled (Psalm 89:34).

In the prophets, assurance and confidence in God was often future oriented. The present and immediate future often presented bleak prospects with grim overtones of judgment, but the distant future was one of great hope, for then Yahweh will come to rule the nations and punish the wicked (Isaiah 2, 11, 13–25, 46–47; Jeremiah 25, 43, 46–51; Ezekiel 25–32, 38–39). Yahweh's coming will usher in a new era in which the promises to the covenant community will be fully realized and their oppression will end. The law of God will be engraved on the hearts of many people (Ezekiel 36:22–31), who will come to know the Lord inwardly and will be brought to a new maturity (Jeremiah 31:31–34); indeed, the whole world will become the beneficiary of the Spirit's redemptive operations, without distinction of race, sex, or class (Joel 2:28–32). Salvation will come to any who call upon Yahweh. God's central covenant promise that sustained his people throughout their history—"ye shall be my people, and I will be your God" (Ezekiel 36:28 KJV)—will reach its culmination in the new age to come.

The Psalms revel in assurance of faith, eliciting confidence in the mercy of a forgiving God, who does not destroy his people even when they fail to trust his saving power (78, 106). The psalmists are assured that Yahweh's mercy is everlasting (136) and that his preservation of his people will not cease (121). Individually, too, the psalmists confess with assurance that Yahweh will deliver them personally from sin, death, condemnation, and all kinds of danger (1, 34). Yahweh is their portion in life, their deliverer in death, and their source of life and joy eternally (16). Despite appalling sorrow at times (22), God's covenant love will follow them all the days of their lives, and they will be with God forever (23:6).

This is not to say, however, that every Old Testament believer always possessed a conscious sense of his or her own assurance of salvation. Certain portions of the Old Covenant, especially some of the Psalms, indicate that even some of the most stalwart believers occasionally lacked assurance, felt the absence of divine favor, and feared—even nearly despaired—that God had cast them off. For example, David (Psalm 38) cried out in confusion, asking why God had withdrawn his favor. In an age where material prosperity was often closely linked with divine benediction, Asaph (Psalm 73) wrestled with the perplexing problem of the poverty of the righteous in the face of the prosperity of the wicked. Heman (Psalm 88), in particular, expresses bleak despondency over the lack of awareness of God's grace amid unrelieved suffering and unmitigated desolation.

Despite assurance not always being present with the Old Covenant believer, the entire testament stresses that assurance was the normal experience of the believer, even if it was often future oriented. Through all the ups and downs of God's children in the Old Covenant, faith relied upon the promises of the covenant God. In the New Covenant, the faith of Old Covenant saints is commended for its assured trust (Hebrews 10:39–12:2). Though revelation and redemption are yet in preparatory stages in the Old Testament and assurance is somewhat more obscure than in the New Testament, the Old Testament believer's assurance of the abiding covenant love of Yahweh differs little from our understanding today of assurance of faith being rooted in the character and promises of God. B. B. Warfield writes:

The reference of faith is accordingly in the Old Testament always distinctly soteriological; its end the Messianic salvation; and its essence a trusting, or rather an entrusting of oneself to the God of salvation, with full assurance of the fulfillment of His gracious purposes and the ultimate realization of His promise of salvation for the people and the individual. Such an attitude towards the God of salvation is identical with the faith of the New Testament, and is not essentially changed by the fuller revelation of God the Redeemer in the person of the promised Messiah.[5]

The Holy Spirit was active in assuring believers in the Old Covenant in all the ways he is active in the New Covenant, though not to the same extent (Westminster Confession of Faith 20.1). Continuity is avowed here, but also novelty, for faith, receiving God's new utterance in the words and deeds of Christ in the New Covenant (Hebrews 1:1–2), becomes a fuller assurance of present salvation (Joel 2:28–32; Acts 2:16–21).

Assurance in the New Testament

In the New Testament, assured faith is viewed as a normative privilege and blessing. The Synoptic Gospels (Matthew, Mark, and Luke) and Acts present faith as assuring trust in the Messiah who grants forgiveness of sins. The design of the Synoptic Gospels is to establish confidence and assurance in the redemptive facts of Christ's ministry, death, and resurrection by showing that the promises are now being fulfilled. The promiser and the promises are now present in the person of the Messiah. Faith is now exercised in the incarnate king whose kingdom is here. Faith now trusts in the living Messiah who has power to heal soul and body—to forgive sins and to heal from every sickness and disease (Mark 2:5; Matthew 9:28); indeed, all things are possible with him (Mark 9:23–24).

The effects of saving faith presented in the Synoptic Gospels are astounding: those who have faith the size of a grain of mustard seed can move mountains (Matthew 17:20). This implies, as Jesus teaches elsewhere more explicitly, that there are varying degrees of faith (Matthew 8:10; Luke 7:9; 17:5). Matthew teaches us that while Jesus reproved "little faith" in his disciples (Matthew 17:20) and commended "great faith" in the centurion (8:10) and the Canaanite woman (15:28), he affirmed that any degree of faith in exercise is sufficient for receiving answers to prayer (21:22).

In the book of Acts, the Pentecostal outpouring of the Spirit fulfils the covenant promises and enriches the fullness of assurance (Joel 2:28–32; Acts 2:16–21). Peter can claim that the promise of universal blessing to Abraham through his seed is now taking place through the resurrection of Christ; in Christ all the families of the earth are being blessed (3:24–26). There is no room for doubt that Jesus is both Lord and Christ (2:36). Now faith is even more focused on the person of Christ. Christ's displays of messianic power in the Synoptic Gospels give way to a fuller concentration on his crucifixion, resurrection, and glorification. Those who have faith are now called believers (2:44; 4:32; 13:38), but the word *faith* is now directed most commonly to the person of Christ (5:14; 9:42; 11:17; 16:31; 18:8; 19:4). Faith in Christ is presented as an assuring commitment to his person, which brings with it salvation both here and hereafter.

The apostle John's writings, especially his gospel and first epistle, point to the full communion with Christ that results from the fiduciary or trusting nature of saving faith. The express purpose of John's Gospel was to promote saving faith in Jesus

Christ (20:31). John's emphasis on coming to Jesus in total self-surrender, on believing in him with full allegiance, and on "eating and drinking him" in radical commitment to him—all point to a fullness of experience that is assuring (6:35–58). Faith in Christ provides an assurance of truly living—both now and in the life to come—through Christ himself, the resurrection and the life (11:25–26).

John's first epistle was written to assure those who have saving faith that they are saved. To do that, John underscores the intimate connection between assurance of salvation and the gift of the Spirit. We are assured of our salvation by the mutual abiding of the Spirit in us and of us in him (3:24; 4:13). That abiding can be known by the ethical accompaniments that flow forth from believers' lives, such as the keeping of God's commandments (2:3–6, 15–17; 3:4–10, 22–24; 4:21; 5:3) and love for fellow believers (3:11–18; 4:7–21).

In Paul's epistles, faith is assured hope based on divine promises that are completed in Christ. Paul affirms repeatedly that he himself possesses this assured hope. Nearly every letter opens with Paul declaring that he is a servant of Jesus Christ; he is an apostle who belongs to Christ and can call him "my God" (1 Corinthians 1:4). He frequently relates how he was converted and from it draws assurance of his own election and final redemption (Galatians 1:15–16; 1 Timothy 1:12–17). He fully expects to be received soon into a state of glorification with Christ (Philippians 1:19–25; 2 Timothy 4:7–8).

Some passages at first glance appear to temper Paul's ready assurance. These passages, however, need to be understood in their contexts. Philippians 3:11–14 should be understood in light of Paul's impending trials and the possibility of his receiving a death sentence (1:8, 12–25). The uncertainty that Paul expressed should therefore be understood in terms of his present earthly life, not of his ultimate salvation. Paul had not yet attained the final perfection of the resurrection and consequently lacked certainty as to whether he would remain alive or go to be with Christ in preparing for that great event. In 1 Corinthians 4:1–5, Paul was not doubting his own salvation, but was recognizing that, in light of the final assize, all human verdicts are ultimately prejudgments. This served as one of his arguments against the factional spirit of the Corinthians, who were far too quick to make rash assessments (1:12–13; 4:6–13). Nor does 1 Corinthians 9:24–27 teach that Paul doubted his own salvation; rather, he was calling the Corinthians to self-examination and watchfulness so as to keep them from the dangers of apostasy.

Paul built his case for assurance of salvation on several grounds:

1. the immutable purpose of God in redemption, who predestines his people to salvation in love (Ephesians 1:4–5)
2. the accomplishment of redemption in Christ (Romans 5:1–11; 2 Corinthians 3:7–18)
3. the believer's union with Christ by faith (Romans 5:12–6:11; 1 Corinthians 6:13–17; 15:12–28; 2 Corinthians 4:7–14; 5:14–17; Ephesians 1)
4. the saving work of the Holy Spirit in applying redemption (Romans 8; 1 Corinthians 12:13; Ephesians 1:13–14)
5. the nature of saving faith as abandonment of all self-merit in fully centering on Christ (Romans 3:22–26; 4:16–25; 8:20–24; 10:5–13; 2 Corinthians 8:5; Galatians 3:21–29)
6. the declarations of God concerning the reward of the faithful, whose good works evidence their saving faith in Christ (2 Corinthians 5:10; 2 Timothy 4:7–8, 14)

Paul's warning passages do not negate that most believers possess assurance. The warnings in Romans 14:15 and 1 Corinthians 8:11 against destroying a weaker believer by offending his or her conscience through an abuse of the principles of Christian liberty deal with the seriousness of overstepping one's conscience, not with the loss of assurance. The warning in 1 Corinthians 11:27–32 about partaking of the Lord's Supper unworthily deals primarily with chastening judgment (11:32), not with loss of assurance. The warning in 10:12 to take heed less one fall is primarily an exhortation to watchfulness rather than a denial of assurance.

In Hebrews, faith is based upon the excellency and finality of Christ's redemptive work, which surpasses the prophets (1:1–3), angels (1:4–14), Moses (3:1–6), Aaron (5:1–10; 7:1–28), and all the high priests of the levitical economy (9:1–10:18). All ninety-six verses of the warning passages in Hebrews are encouragements to persevere in the faith in the midst of difficulties and discouragements; none of them denies perseverance or assurance. The author reminds the Hebrew Christians that though he warns them not to fall into presumption or unbelief, he is persuaded of better things for them (6:9). He invites them to enter the most holy place (formerly restricted to an annual visit by the high priest) of the New Covenant, with full confidence and assurance of faith, trusting in Christ's accomplished redemption alone (10:19–22).

James stresses that faith is antithetical to doubt. Faith is single-mindedness; doubt is double-mindedness (1:5–8). Faith shows its reality by producing good works; assurance of salvation is confirmed by the presence of good works and is strengthened through enduring trials patiently for Christ's sake (1:4, 12; 2:18–26).

Peter's epistles show faith as trustful hope that ushers in love and joy. Faith is always directed to Christ, always looking forward to the final consummation. Meanwhile, the believer is preserved "by the power of God through faith unto salvation" for an indestructible inheritance (1 Peter 1:3–12 KJV). Nothing can destroy the assurance of that faith—not even trials or persecutions, which, in fact, help the believer identify with Christ and thereby factor into God's saving purposes (4:12–14).

Second Peter stresses that the believer does not gain assurance by looking at oneself or at anything one has produced apart from God's promises, but primarily by looking to God's faithfulness in Christ as he is revealed in the gospel's promises (1:3–4). The same promises that lead to salvation are sufficient to lead the believer to assurance. As assurance grows, God's promises become increasingly real and meaningful to the believer.

The New Testament, particularly in its repeated admonitions to seek assurance, also acknowledges the possible lack of assurance in the Christian's life. Peter urges: "Give diligence to make your calling and election sure" (2 Peter 1:10 KJV). Paul tells the Corinthians that they should examine themselves as to whether they are in the faith (2 Corinthians 13:5). The first epistle of John repeatedly shows how believers may know that they know God (1 John 1:7; 2:3, 5, 23, 27; 3:14, 19; 4:13; 5:2, 13). And the writer of Hebrews exhorts his readers to "draw near with a true heart in full assurance of faith" (10:22 KJV), implying that there were those who were experiencing less than full assurance of faith. All of this, however, is not to deny that the roots of assurance lie in saving faith, which by its very nature cannot doubt. Assurance in both the Old and New Covenant is normative for believers, though not every believer possesses large measures of it.

In sum, the very character of the New Covenant, based on Christ's death and resurrection and on the Spirit's indwelling, indicates that assurance must be a constitutive element of saving faith. Whatever form assurance takes in different stages of redemptive revelation, it appears to coalesce with faith. This is supported by concepts such as the fidelity of God, the truth of his promise, the centrality of Christ and his mediatorial work, the infallible testimony of the Holy Spirit, the radical nature of salvation, and the sovereignty of grace.

Justification of Believers under the Old Testament

Today, the question is often asked: Were the Old Testament saints justified by grace alone through faith in Christ? In actuality, the question answers itself. If their justification was not by grace alone through faith, then how else were they justified? The Bible does not acknowledge any other way for a sinner to be saved (Psalm 130:3; 143:2). Even so, more than one theologian has attempted to set the New Testament in opposition to the Old, implying that the Old Testament saints were justified by works of the law or, at most, experienced only a very limited form of the gratuitous justification granted to believers under the New Testament.

These attempts to separate the testaments fly in the face of the biblical witness to the unity of the covenant of grace, revealed in seed form as the protevangelium (Genesis 3:15) to Adam and subsequently restated to Noah, given in explicit form as the covenant made with Abraham, attested and confirmed by the testimonies and ceremonies of the Mosaic law, and finally renewed, ratified, and fulfilled by the shedding of the blood of Christ. "There are not, therefore, two covenants of grace differing in substance, but one and the same under various dispensations" (Westminster Confession of Faith 7.6).

Even more telling against such attempts is the way in which New Testament writers construct the doctrine of justification entirely out of Old Testament materials. The apostle Paul insists that "the righteousness of God without the law is manifested, being witnessed by the law and the prophets; even the righteousness of God which is by faith of Jesus Christ unto all and upon all them that believe" (Romans 3:21–22 KJV). The apostles did not have to invent a new doctrine of justification. They found one ready at hand in the Scriptures of the Old Testament, exhibited in the ceremonies of the law, expounded by the prophets, and woven into the fabric of the spiritual experience of the Old Testament saints.

Paul thus devotes much attention to the history of Abraham (Romans 4; Galatians 3), presenting him as "the father of all them that believe, though they be not circumcised, that righteousness may be imputed to them also: and the father of circumcision to them who are not of the circumcision only, but who also walk in the steps of that faith of our father Abraham, which he had being yet uncircumcised" (Romans 4:11–12 KJV). He assures the Galatian believers: "Ye are all the children of God by faith in Christ Jesus. . . . And if ye be Christ's, then are ye Abraham's seed, and heirs according to the promise" (Galatians 3:26, 29 KJV).

For his doctrine of the imputation of Christ's righteousness to all who believe in him—the foundation of the doctrine of justification by faith alone—the apostle turns to David. "David also describeth the blessedness of the man, unto whom God imputeth righteousness without works," writes Paul (Romans 4:6 KJV), citing Psalm 32:1–2. The history of David lends itself especially well to Paul's purposes. David was a notorious sinner, and there is no more heartfelt or explicit presentation of the biblical doctrine of sin, both original and actual, than Psalm 51, while in Psalm 32 David makes it clear that he himself is the "blessed . . . man to whom the Lord will not impute sin" (Romans 4:8 KJV).

Since therefore the apostles derived all the essential ideas and even the necessary vocabulary for their doctrine of justification from the experience and witness of the Old Testament saints, it is right to conclude that "the justification of believers under the Old Testament was, in all these respects, one and the same with the justification of believers under the New Testament" (Westminster Confession of Faith 11.6). They were justified by their faith in the promised Messiah, whose atoning work was revealed in the ceremonies of the law and whose power to save was heralded by the prophets. In that Messiah they had, as believers today have, "full remission of sins and eternal salvation" (7.5).

Conclusion

Scripture shows that assurance of salvation ought to be regarded as the possession of all Christians in principle, despite varying measures of consciousness. Passages such as Psalm 88 warn us not to deny our redemption if we temporarily lack assurance. Assurance for believers is normal, but that normativity does not make it essential at all times. The lack of assurance ought to direct us to Scripture's stress on the ministry of the Word, the Spirit, and the sacraments in cultivating assuring faith within the covenantal community of the living church.

Assurance is covenantally based, sealed with the blood of Christ, and grounded ultimately in eternal election. Though assurance remains incomplete in this life, varies in degree, and is often assaulted by affliction and doubt, its riches must never be taken for granted. It is both a gift, for it is always the gracious and sovereign gift of the Triune God, and a pursuit, for it must be sought diligently through the means of grace. It becomes well grounded only when it evidences fruits and marks of grace such as love to God and for his kingdom, filial obedience, godly repentance, hatred for sin, love for believers, and humble adoration. Assurance produces holy living marked by spiritual peace, joyful love, humble gratitude, and cheerful obedience. Happily, these marks and fruits of grace are also the fruit of Christ's redemption received by faith through grace.

7

The Glory of True Repentance

John MacArthur

I speak affectionately to the weaker ones, who cannot yet say that they know they have believed. I speak not to your condemnation, but to your consolation. Full assurance is not essential to salvation, but it is essential to satisfaction. May you get—may you get it at once; at any rate may you never be satisfied to live without it. You may have full assurance. You may have it without personal revelations: it is wrought in us by the Word of God.

—Charles H. Spurgeon, "The Blessing of Full Assurance"

You might wonder why a book on assurance includes a chapter that gives special prominence to repentance. It is because one of the first things that *ought* to be evident in the life of every genuine believer is a spirit of heartfelt contrition over sin. In a vital sense, repentance is one of the initial, essential, and most definitive evidences that authentic conversion has indeed taken place.

When Cornelius was converted in Acts 10, the conclusive, insurmountable proof that he was well and truly saved was his repentance. Jewish believers in the Jerusalem church found it difficult to imagine that God would save a Gentile unless the Gentile first became a proselyte to Judaism. Many who had been schooled all their lives in Old Testament law naturally expected Gentile Christians to submit to the ritual of circumcision and put themselves under all the ceremonial and dietary laws of the Old Testament. But the immediate fruit of Cornelius's repentance was a convincing and irrefutable confirmation that he had been accepted by Christ *as a Gentile*: "When they heard this, they quieted down and glorified God, saying, 'Well then, God has granted to the Gentiles also the repentance that leads to life'" (11:18 NASB).

Likewise, the dramatic repentance of the Thessalonians was sufficient proof for the apostle Paul to conclude that they had sincerely received the Word of God—and not in vain (1 Thessalonians 1:5–6). The Thessalonians' well-known repentance was also the basis of their testimony to the surrounding regions. Everyone was talking about it, Paul said: "For they themselves report about us what kind of a reception we had with you, and how you turned to God from idols to serve a living and true God" (1:9 NASB).

Over the years, I have ministered quite a lot in Russia, the Ukraine, Belarus, and other parts of the former Soviet Union. The church in those countries, repressed by Communism for so many decades, is nonetheless vibrant and dynamic today. One of the significant things that struck me when I first began to minister there was the terminology that virtually all Russian-speaking believers use to describe conversion. They do not speak of accepting Christ as one's personal Savior. They would never say merely that someone "made a decision for Christ" or that the person "invited Jesus into his or her life." The language they use is simple and entirely biblical: the new believer is someone who has *repented*. If a person shows no evidence of repentance, he or she would not be embraced as a Christian, no matter what sort of verbal profession of faith was made.

Moreover, in those churches, when a person repents, he or she is expected to express repentance verbally to the church. The new believer is asked to stand before the whole church and confess guilt and renounce sin. Until the believer has done that, no one takes it for granted that he or she has sincerely repented. In effect, then, public expression of repentance is a prerequisite for formal membership in the church.

By contrast, we live in a culture of such shallow religion that most of what goes by the name "Christian" in Western society has little or no emphasis on repentance of any kind. The call to repentance has been deliberately omitted from the most popular gospel presentations of our generation. As a result, multitudes of people nowadays think of themselves as Christians but have never truly repented. In many cases, they know next to nothing about repentance, because the subject is almost never brought up in contemporary evangelistic preaching, in personal evangelism, or even in the regular teaching of the church. (It seems that many churches are too concerned with being "seeker sensitive" and not committed enough to proclaiming the whole counsel of God clearly.)

Contemporary evangelicalism has therefore welcomed into the fold countless unrepentant people who have never once entertained a serious thought about sin but nonetheless profess to

127

know Christ, use his name, claim assurance of eternal life, hold formal membership in the church, and are absolutely confident that they have need of nothing more in the spiritual realm. According to Scripture, that is a deadly *false* assurance.

A sound understanding of repentance would disabuse most such people of their false assurance, and that is why a good look at what Scripture says about repentance is fitting for a book on the doctrine of assurance.

What Is Repentance?

There is a great deal of confusion these days about what Scripture means by the expression *repentance*. The Greek word for "repentance" is *metanoia*, from *meta* ("after") and *noeo* ("to understand"). Literally it means "an afterthought" or "a change of mind," and some insist that this is all the word means—a shift in one's way of thinking, with no necessary moral ramifications whatsoever. One very popular school of theological thought claims that biblical repentance is simply a new perspective about who Jesus is. In other words, repentance is just another word for believing. Thus it is not really necessary to speak of repentance as something distinct from faith. That view became popular, if not dominant, in the popular American evangelicalism of the twentieth century, and it is the major reason that repentance—both the concept and the word—has all but disappeared from the gospel vocabulary of the evangelical movement in the Western hemisphere.

But the true meaning of any term must be defined by how it is used in Scripture and not merely by an appeal to the strict literal sense of the Greek word derivation. Context, not just etymology, is the key. Here's what one of the best dictionaries of New Testament terminology says about the word *repentance*:

"The predominantly intellectual understanding of *metanoia* as a change of mind plays very little part in the NT. Rather the decision by the whole man to turn round is stressed. It is clear that we are concerned neither with a purely outward turning nor with a merely intellectual change of ideas."[1] Another standard resource on New Testament word usage says *metanoia* describes a "radical conversion, a transformation of nature, a definitive turning from evil, a resolute turning to God in total obedience (Mk. 1:15; Mt. 4:17; 18:3). . . . It affects the whole man, first and basically the centre of personal life, then logically his conduct at all times and in all situations, his thoughts, words and acts."[2] And Thayer defines *metanoia* as "the change of mind of those who have begun to abhor their errors and misdeeds, and have determined to enter upon a better course of life, so that it embraces both a recognition of sin and sorrow for it and hearty amendment, the tokens and effects of which are good deeds."[3]

In other words, when the New Testament speaks of repentance, it *always* describes a complete renovation of purpose, a wholesale change of heart, an absolute moral about-face, a definite renunciation of the old ways—and specifically a deliberate turning from sin. Repentance as Jesus described it involves repudiation of self, disavowal of sin, and turning to God for salvation (Matthew 10:37–39; 16:24–26). There is no legitimate way to reduce the biblical concept of repentance to a discreet, academic mind maneuver.

There is, obviously, a true sense in which a radical change of mind is at the very heart of true repentance. But clearly it is much more than the casual adoption of a new perspective on some intellectual or academic point of doctrine. Notice again how the apostle Paul described the repentance of the Thessalonian believers: "You turned to God from idols to serve a living and true God" (1 Thessalonians 1:9 NASB). He outlines three vital elements of all genuine repentance: a turning to God, a turning from sin, with the purpose of serving God. True repentance includes all those elements; it is folly to think of repentance as merely a passive change of opinion about Christ. It is, in fact, a radical heart change that inevitably affects behavior as well.

That is not to suggest that repentance itself is a change of behavior rather than a change of mind. Repentance is not like the Roman Catholic notion of penance, where attempts are made to atone for one's own sin. Nor is repentance merely shame or sorrow for sin. In fact, according to 2 Corinthians 7:10, repentance is sometimes motivated by a profound godly sorrow when the Holy Spirit convicts of sin. But the sorrow itself is not true repentance. On the other hand, genuine repentance does necessarily involve an element of remorse. A person has not really turned from sin until hating it in oneself and mourning its effects in one's life. This is precisely the kind of mourning that Jesus was describing in the Beatitudes: "Blessed are those who mourn, for they shall be comforted" (Matthew 5:4 NASB).

Again, repentance is a wholesale change of purpose and perspective, with particular relevance to sin and to God. It is a turning from sin and a corresponding turning toward God. It results in a redirection of the human will, involving a purposeful intention to forsake unrighteousness and pursue righteousness instead.

But authentic repentance cannot be manufactured by the sinner's own heart, evoked by a simple decision, or conjured up by emotional manipulation. As a matter of fact, Scripture explicitly teaches that sinners have no power to produce repentance in their own hearts: "Can the Ethiopian change his skin / or the leopard his spots? / Then you also can do good / who are accustomed to doing evil" (Jeremiah 13:23 NASB). "Because the mind set on the flesh is hostile toward God; for it does not subject itself to the law of God, for it is not even able to do so, and those who are in the flesh cannot please God" (Romans 8:7–8 NASB).

If repentance is not an attitude that can be summoned out of a disobedient heart by sheer willpower alone, it must not be thought of as a human work. It is a gracious work of God in the sinner. Think again about the implications of Acts 11:18 and the early Jewish believers' response to Cornelius's conversion: "*God* has granted to the Gentiles also the repentance that leads to life" (NASB).

Authentic repentance is a divine gift. That is why Paul urged Timothy to correct those who oppose the truth: "If perhaps *God may grant them repentance* leading to the knowledge of the truth" (2 Timothy 2:25 NASB). If God sovereignly bestows repentance as a gift, we should never think of it as merely a product of human emotions or the human will.

That also means we should never think of repentance as an attempt to clean up one's own life and behavior before coming to Christ for salvation. When Christ demanded repentance, he was not calling sinners to self-reform. In fact, authentic repentance begins with the sinner's recognition that one is hopelessly in bondage to sin and powerless to change. Jesus's classic example of repentance was a tax gatherer who came to understand his hopeless situation. He was so deeply ashamed of his sin that he kept his distance from the holy place in the temple. He was so profoundly humbled by the weight of his own guilt that he dared not even raise his face to heaven. But he simply smote his breast (signifying grief over his sinfulness) and pleaded with God for mercy (Luke 18:13). Jesus said he "went to his house justified" (18:14 NASB). *God* granted him authentic repentance.

This publican's conversion demonstrates how repentance is far more than a simple adjustment of one's opinions about Christ. There was nothing casual or perfunctory about the publican's state of mind. This was not an idle change of mind, but a redirection of the man's whole self as he came to hate sin and love God. In the words of well-known Dutch Reformed theologian Geerhardus Vos:

> Our Lord's idea of repentance is as profound and comprehensive as his conception of righteousness. Of the three words that are used in the Greek Gospels to describe the process, one emphasizes the emotional element of regret, sorrow over the past evil course of life, *metamelomai*; Matt. 21:2–32; a second expresses reversal of the entire mental attitude, *metanoe*; Matt. 12:41, Luke 11:32; 15:7, 10; the third denotes a change in the direction of life, one goal being substituted for another, *epistrephomai*; Matt. 13:15 (and parallels); Luke 17:4; 22:32. Repentance is not limited to any single faculty of the mind: it engages the entire man, intellect, will and affections. . . . Again, in the new life, which follows repentance, the absolute supremacy of God is the controlling principle. He who repents turns away from the service of mammon and self to the service of God.[4]

So while there is no question that repentance involves a change of mind, it certainly does not end there. It is a wholesale change in direction, a change in purpose, a change in attitude, and a change of affections. All of this can be the result of only God's gracious regenerating work and is therefore evidence of true salvation.

To look at the same point from a different angle—all of salvation is God's work, and he would not omit the vital work of repentance. Therefore, if all the fruits of authentic repentance are absent from a person's life, there is good reason to doubt that person's salvation. That is precisely what John the Baptist said when a group of Pharisees and Sadducees came to him to be baptized. He demanded to see proof of their repentance: "You brood of vipers, who warned you to flee from the wrath to come? Therefore bear fruit in keeping with repentance" (Matthew 3:7–8 NASB). He knew that if their repentance was genuine, the evidence of it would be visible in their behavior.

Examining the Fruits of Repentance

What kind of evidence substantiates authentic repentance? When the crowds asked that question of John the Baptist in Luke 3:10, he told them to share with their needy neighbors (3:11). To tax collectors, he said: "Collect no more than what you have been ordered to" (3:13 NASB). To soldiers, he said: "Do not take money from anyone by force, or accuse anyone falsely, and be content with your wages" (3:14 NASB). In each case, John was calling for a selfless attitude and kindness to one's neighbors. His short list of three items does not exhaust all the possible fruits of repentance, of course, but it demonstrates that genuine repentance ought to produce the kind of character change that results in a qualitative difference in the way we live. James wrote: "Faith without works is dead" (2:26 NASB). In a similar way, repentance that does not produce works is barren and useless. A person who has genuinely repented is never left unchanged.

The apostle Paul likewise looked for proof of repentance: "I did not prove disobedient to the heavenly vision, but kept declaring . . . to the Gentiles, that they should repent and turn to God, *performing deeds appropriate to repentance*" (Acts 26:19–20 NASB).

133

Jesus told a parable that illustrates the hypocrisy of a profession of faith without repentance: "What do you think? A
man had two sons, and he came to the first and said, 'Son, go
work today in the vineyard.' And he answered, 'I will not'; but
afterward he regretted it and went. The man came to the second
and said the same thing; and he answered, 'I will, sir'; but he did
not go. Which of the two did the will of his father?" (Matthew
21:28–31 NASB). The answer is obvious: the one who went.
His obedience was the irrefutable evidence of his repentance.
The other son's profession meant nothing in the absence of
obedience. Faith without works is dead. Repentance without
fruit means nothing.

This emphasis is consistent throughout Scripture. Repentance is a gift from God. It is the first indication that regeneration
has taken place: "If anyone is in Christ, he is a new creature;
the old things passed away; behold, new things have come"
(2 Corinthians 5:17 NASB). That is why Scripture presents
self-examination as an essential prerequisite for authentic assurance (13:5). The evidences of true salvation cited in Scripture
include the fruits of one's behavior (1 John 3:18–19), pattern
of life (3:24), and way of thinking (5:1–2).

Do not be misled: salvation is in no way merited by our
works, and therefore true assurance is not ultimately grounded
in our performance. The ultimate ground and foundation of
all true assurance is the promise of salvation to all who believe.
That promise is as true as God himself and needs no empirical
verification.

As we have seen, however, the fruits of repentance are the
true test of whether our faith is authentic. Thus self-examination is a necessary aspect of gaining true assurance. But it is
not the end-all of assurance. Self-examination can destroy false
assurance, but we will never derive settled assurance merely by

looking at ourselves. In the end, we have to look away from self and rest in the objective promises of God's Word. If we seek to anchor our assurance in our own performance rather than in God's promises, we will never know full assurance.

Still, self-examination is a necessary and biblical aspect of gaining assurance. It is the process by which we evaluate the quality of our own faith, and the fruit of repentance is the evidence we must seek. This is especially crucial in the contemporary evangelical environment. Multitudes believe that they are saved merely because someone told them so after a cursory conversation, the simple reciting of a canned prayer, the raising of a hand in a public meeting, or sometimes even less. People have not been challenged to examine themselves. Rarely do they test their assurance by God's Word. As a matter of fact, many have been taught that doubts about their salvation can only be detrimental to spiritual health and growth.

But Scripture *demands* self-examination. In fact, we are supposed to examine ourselves regularly, every time we partake of the Lord's Supper (1 Corinthians 11:28). Paul's famous challenge to the believers at Corinth clearly has the doctrine of assurance in view: "Test yourselves *to see if you are in the faith*; examine yourselves! Or do you not recognize this about yourselves, that Jesus Christ is in you—unless indeed you fail the test?" (2 Corinthians 13:5 NASB). And Hebrews 10:22 indicates that "full assurance of faith" comes from "having our hearts sprinkled clean from an evil conscience" (NASB).

So we need to examine ourselves in the process of coming to grips with assurance. Nowhere in Scripture is this more plain than in 1 John, which is one of the key passages of Scripture on the subject of assurance. In fact, the epistle was written with the express purpose of building the assurance of true believers: "These things I have written to you who believe in the name of the Son of God, so that you may know that you have eternal life" (1 John 5:13 NASB). His aim is to deepen the assurance of genuine Christians—those "who believe in the name of the Son of God." He is not trying to provoke doubts in the presence of authentic faith; he is giving us a basis to "assure our heart before Him" (3:19 NASB). Notice again, however, that our faith in Christ is the ultimate ground and foundation of true assurance. Self-examination is simply the process by which we examine whether our faith is genuine and our repentance real.

True believers should not be unnerved by the biblical call to self-examination. Unbelievers and mere hearers of the Word, on the other hand, *need* to have their self-confidence shaken. So the apostle John names several practical tests that may be used to determine the authenticity of faith—including such things as obedience (1 John 2:3–6; 3:1–10), sound doctrine (2:21–28; 4:1–6), and love for believers (3:14–19; 4:7–11). Those are fruits of true repentance.

Dealing with Sin in the Believer's Life

The apostle John, of course, recognizes that believers do fail and fall into sin. As a matter of fact, he began the epistle with a series of statements underscoring the truth that no one can claim any degree of perfection in this life: "If we say that we have no sin, we are deceiving ourselves and the truth is not in us. . . . If we say that we have not sinned, we make Him a liar and His word is not in us" (1 John 1:8, 10 NASB). When we sin, however, Christ is our advocate with the Father (2:1) as well as the all-sufficient sacrifice who has paid the price for our sin (2:2).

Therefore, we *can* know true assurance, despite the sinful and fleshly tendencies we all struggle with. Paul testifies in Romans 7 about his own frustrating battle to overcome the sin that remains in each one of us as long as we inhabit fallen flesh. We all sin all the time, and we wage the very same struggle that Paul describes in 7:14–24. But Paul ends his discussion with a celebration of his own assurance ("thanks be to God through Jesus Christ our Lord!"; 7:25 NASB), and then he devotes the entirety of Romans 8 to a discourse about the believer's security in the Spirit.

How can believers know that kind of assurance, even while being aware of their own sinfulness? First, it is vital to understand that Scripture expressly refutes all forms of perfectionism. Even when the apostle John writes, "No one who is born of God practices sin, because His seed abides in him; and he cannot sin, because he is born of God" (1 John 3:9 NASB), he is clearly not making perfection a test of salvation, because he recognizes and even emphasizes the inevitability of sin in every believer's life.

The point of 1 John 3:9 has to do with our attitude toward sin and righteousness, our heart's response when we *do* sin, and the overall direction of our walk. In other words, we do not test the genuineness of our repentance by the *perfection* of our walk, but by the *direction* of it. In the words of Puritan John Owen: "Your state is not at all to be measured by the opposition that sin makes to you, but by the opposition you make to it."[5]

What is the true moral object of your affections? Is it sin or righteousness? If your chief love is sin, then according to the principles outlined in 1 John you are "of the devil" (3:8, 10). If you love righteousness and practice righteousness, you are born of God (2:29). This is not measured by the frequency, duration, or magnitude of one's sins, but by the inclination of the heart.

The true mark of a redeemed heart is a spirit of repentance, mourning over our sin when we do fall, and a deep and abiding dependence on God's grace as we wage the warfare against sin.

To quote Owen once more: "A man, then, may have a deep sense of sin all his days, walk under the sense of it continually, abhor himself for his ingratitude, unbelief, and rebellion against God, without any impeachment of his assurance."[6] That may sound preposterous, but an understanding of the depth of our own sin is the very thing that keeps Christians from falling into utter despair. We *know* we are guilty, fallen, and frail. To use the exact idea conveyed in the Greek text of 1 John 1:9, we agree with God about our sin. When we discover sin in our lives, we are not shocked or astonished, but we nonetheless hate that it is there. We trust Christ, our advocate, for forgiveness and cleansing. And far from becoming tolerant or comfortable with sin in our lives, we become more and more determined to mortify it. In the words of the apostle: "I am writing these things to you *so that you may not sin*" (2:1 NASB).

In other words, a spirit of perpetual repentance ought to permeate and characterize the life of every true believer. The repentance that takes place at conversion begins a progressive, lifelong process of confession and forgiveness (1:9). That spirit of continual repentance in no way undermines the assurance of a true child of God. On the contrary, it is the very thing that feeds our assurance and keeps it alive.

8

GOD'S MEANS
OF ASSURANCE

Keith A. Mathison

It is not God's design that men should obtain assurance in any other way, than by mortifying corruption, increasing in grace, and obtaining the lively exercises of it. And although self-examination be a duty of great use and importance, and by no means to be neglected; yet it is not the principal means, by which the saints do get satisfaction of their good estate. Assurance is not to be obtained so much by self-examination, as by action. The apostle Paul sought assurance chiefly this way, even by forgetting the things that were behind, and reaching forth, unto those things that were before, pressing towards the mark for the prize of the high calling of God in Christ Jesus; if by any means he might attain unto the resurrection of the dead. And it was by this means chiefly that he obtained assurance (1 Cor. 9:26). "I therefore so run, as not uncertainly." He obtained assurance of winning the prize more by running than by considering.

—Jonathan Edwards, *Religious Affections*

"I believe; help my unbelief!" (Mark 9:24). Such was the cry to Jesus by the desperate father of a demon-afflicted child, but it has also been the cry of many Christians throughout the centuries. A true Christian, by definition, is one who has faith, but the faith of many true Christians is a weak faith (Romans 14:1). And because the faith of many Christians is weak, their assurance of salvation is also weak. The need of such Christians, and of all Christians, is to have their faith continually strengthened as they grow in grace. But how are Christians to strengthen their faith and thus their assurance? How are they to grow in grace? The answer is the means of grace that God has provided for his people.

What are the means of grace? The Westminster Shorter Catechism provides a concise description: "The outward and ordinary means whereby Christ communicateth to us the benefits of redemption, are his ordinances, especially the word, sacraments, and prayer; all which are made effectual to the elect for salvation" (A. 88). From this definition, we understand that there are several means of grace: the Word, sacraments, and prayer. These means of grace are, as the catechism explains, the channels through which Christ communicates to his people the benefits of redemption.[1] God uses these means, as John Calvin explains, to "increase faith within us, and advance it to its goal."[2] Just as food is a means of physical growth, the Word, sacraments, and prayer are the means of spiritual growth.

The Word as a Means of Grace

The first and primary means of grace is the Word of God, in particular the preaching of the Word. The Westminster Larger Catechism explains how the Word is used by God as a means of grace:

The Spirit of God maketh the reading, but especially the preaching of the word, an effectual means of enlightening, convincing, and humbling sinners; of driving them out of themselves, and drawing them unto Christ; of conforming them to his image, and subduing them to his will; of strengthening them against temptations and corruptions; of building them up in grace, and establishing their hearts in holiness and comfort through faith unto salvation. (A. 155)

The power of the Word to accomplish these things is emphasized repeatedly in Scripture (Psalm 19:7; Jeremiah 23:29; John 17:17; Romans 1:16; 1 Corinthians 1:23–24; 2 Timothy 3:14–17; Hebrews 4:12).

It was by means of God's mighty Word that he created out of nothing all that exists (Genesis 1). And it is by means of his Word that he sanctifies his people. The Word of God declares God's law, revealing his will and convicting humanity of sin. The Word of God also declares the gospel, calling humanity to faith. For those who believe, the Word of God enables their continued growth in grace. Charles Hodge explains:

It is obvious that we can have no rational feelings of gratitude, love, adoration and fear toward God, except in view of the truths revealed concerning Him in His Word. We can have no love or devotion to Christ, except so far as the manifestation of His character and work is accepted by us as true. We can have no faith except as founded on some revealed promise of God; no resignation or submission except in view of the wisdom and love of God and of His universal providence as revealed in the Scriptures; no joyful anticipation of future blessedness which is not founded on what the Gospel makes known of a future state of existence.[3]

In other words, we grow in our faith, hope, and love as we come to understand more and more of what God has revealed in his Word about himself, his redemptive work, and his promises.

The Westminster Confession of Faith accurately describes Scripture as "most necessary" (1.1). It is necessary for our salvation, for apart from the Word of God, we would not know the gospel, which we must hear and believe in order to be saved (Romans 10:13–17). Scripture is necessary for our continued sanctification. Jesus himself declared that we are to live "by every word that comes from the mouth of God" (Matthew 4:4). Calvin explains how the Word sustains us.

> To maintain us in this spiritual life, the thing requisite is not to feed our bodies with fading and corruptible food, but to nourish our souls on the best and most precious diet. Now all Scripture tells us, that the spiritual food by which our souls are maintained is that same word by which the Lord has regenerated us; but it frequently adds the reason, viz., that in it Jesus Christ, our only life, is given and administered to us. For we must not imagine that there is life anywhere than in God. But just as God has placed all fullness of life in Jesus, in order to communicate it to us by his means, so he ordained his word as the instrument by which Jesus Christ, with all his graces, is dispensed to us. Still it always remains true, that our souls have no other pasture than Jesus Christ. Our heavenly Father, therefore, in his care to nourish us, gives us no other, but rather recommends us to take our fill there, as a refreshment amply sufficient, with which we cannot dispense, and beyond which no other can be found.[4]

As Peter explains, the Word of God is the "pure spiritual milk" that nourishes believers (1 Peter 2:2). The Word is also necessary for those who would walk according to God's will, for it is impossible to follow his will if we do not know his will, and his will for us is revealed in his Word (1 John 5:3).

It is important to understand that in order for the Word to be efficacious, the Holy Spirit must work by and with the Word in the hearts of people. Clarifying the difference between the Reformed doctrine and the Lutheran doctrine, Robert Reymond explains: "The Reformed position on the efficacy of the Word as a means of grace is that, even though the Bible is the very Word of God, it is rendered efficacious as a means of special grace, not intrinsically or automatically, but only by the immediate and direct attendant working of the Holy Spirit in the hearts of its readers and hearers."[5]

All Scripture is God breathed. All Scripture is the Word of the living God. Those who would grow in grace and have their faith and assurance strengthened will make every effort to avail themselves of this means of grace. They will joyfully sit under the faithful preaching of the Word (Nehemiah 8:7–8; Acts 18:11; 20:26–27). They will prayerfully read and meditate upon the Word of God, searching the Scriptures and seeking the illumination of the Holy Spirit (Acts 17:11). They will not be only hearers of the Word, but doers as well (James 1:22–25). By means of the Word of truth they will be sanctified (John 17:17).

Sacraments as Means of Grace

The sacraments of baptism and the Lord's Supper are the second means of grace provided by God.[6] The Westminster Larger Catechism helpfully defines a sacrament as "an holy ordinance instituted by Christ in his church, to signify, seal, and exhibit unto those that are within the covenant of grace, the benefits of his mediation; to strengthen and increase their faith, and all other graces; to oblige them to obedience; to testify and cherish their love and communion one with another; and to distinguish them from those that are without" (A. 162). The sacraments "become effectual means of salvation, not by any power in themselves, or any virtue derived from the piety or intention of him by whom they are administered, but only by the working of the Holy Ghost, and the blessing of Christ, by whom they are instituted" (A. 161). The Westminster Shorter Catechism adds that the sacraments become effectual means of salvation only "in them that by faith receive them" (A. 91).

The Reformed doctrine of the sacraments set forth in the Westminster standards is contrasted with Roman Catholic doctrine, which insists that the sacraments work *ex opere operato*, that is, by virtue of the work being performed. According to Roman Catholic doctrine, when the sacraments are celebrated properly, the grace they signify is always made efficaciously present.[7] According to the Reformed doctrine, the sacraments are not intrinsically efficacious. Their efficacy requires that the Holy Spirit be at work in and through them and that they be received in faith.

The Reformed doctrine of the sacraments is also contrasted with the Zwinglian doctrine, which understands the sacraments to be merely symbols of spiritual truths. According to the Reformed doctrine, the sacraments consist of three aspects: the visible elements and actions (the signs), the spiritual reality (the things signified), and the spiritual relation (the sacramental union) between the signs and the things signified (Westminster Confession of Faith 27.2). Because of the sacramental union established by God, the sacraments effectually confer grace to those who receive them in faith.[8] As several Reformed confessions indicate, for those with faith God performs spiritually what the sacraments signify physically (Belgic Confession §§34–35; French Confession §37).

Baptism

Baptism is defined by the Westminster Confession of Faith as

> a sacrament of the New Testament, ordained by Jesus Christ, not only for the solemn admission of the party baptized into the visible Church, but also to be unto him a sign and seal of the covenant of grace, of his ingrafting into Christ, of regeneration, of remission of sins, and of his giving up unto God, through Jesus Christ, to walk in newness of life: which sacrament is, by Christ's own appointment, to be continued in his Church until the end of the world. . . .
>
> The efficacy of baptism is not tied to that moment of time wherein it is administered; yet, notwithstanding, by the right use of this ordinance, the grace promised is not only offered, but really exhibited and conferred by the Holy Ghost, to such (whether of age or infants) as that grace belongeth unto, according to the counsel of God's own will, in his appointed time. (28.1, 6)

Baptism, then, is a sign and seal in which the grace of God is exhibited and conferred by the Holy Spirit to such as that grace belongs. In order to understand what this means, it is helpful to examine the function of circumcision as a sign and seal of the covenant made with Abraham. When God called Abram out of Ur, he made a number of promises to Abram (Genesis 12:1–3). God promised that he would bless Abram, that he would make Abram's name great, and that through Abram all the nations of the earth would be blessed. In Genesis 15, God formally inaugurates his covenant with Abram. God promises Abram a son, and because Abram believes God, God counts it to him as righteousness (15:6). God also promises Abram that he will give him the land of Canaan to possess, and when Abram asks how he is to know that he will possess the land, God's response is in the form of a covenant ceremony (15:9–18).

In Genesis 17, God confirms the covenant he made with Abram by changing Abram's name to Abraham and by instituting circumcision as the sign and seal of the covenant (17:11). Circumcision both symbolized and necessitated a corresponding cleansing of the heart (Leviticus 26:41; Deuteronomy 10:16; Jeremiah 4:4; 9:25–26). Circumcision did not, however, automatically effect this internal change, otherwise God would not call those who had been circumcised in the flesh to be circumcised also in their heart. Faith was required in order for the internal change to be effected. Abraham experienced the inner change, the circumcision of the heart, before he was given the outward sign of that change. For Abraham, circumcision was a seal of his already existing faith (Romans 4:10–12). His son Isaac, on the other hand, received the outward sign of inward purification when he was only eight days old (Genesis 21:4). The reception of this outward sign did not automatically confer upon him the inner purification that it signified. Instead, the outward sign of circumcision placed a requirement on Isaac to be circumcised in his heart, to exercise true faith in God.

Baptism functions as a means of grace both as a sign and as a seal. It visibly signifies the believer's union with Christ, the believer's regeneration, and the remission of the believer's sin. It is a visible word testifying to the truth of those realities. It is also a seal, confirming God's covenantal promises. To those with faith, the spiritual realities promised in the sacraments are "not only offered, but really exhibited and conferred by the Holy Ghost" (Westminster Confession of Faith 28.6). The Belgic Confession (1561) explains: "The Ministers, on their part, administer the Sacrament, and that which is visible, but our

Lord giveth that which is signified by the Sacrament, namely, the gifts and invisible grace" (§34).

Lord's Supper

Our Lord Jesus Christ has also provided the sacrament of the Lord's Supper as a means of grace.[9] The Westminster Larger Catechism defines the Lord's Supper as

> a sacrament of the New Testament, wherein, by giving and receiving bread and wine according to the appointment of Jesus Christ, his death is shewed forth; and they that worthily communicate feed upon his body and blood, to their spiritual nourishment and growth in grace; have their union and communion with him confirmed; testify and renew their thankfulness, and engagement to God, and their mutual love and fellowship each with other, as members of the same mystical body. (A. 168)

In Scripture, a variety of terms refer to this sacrament: "breaking of bread" (Acts 2:42), "communion" (1 Corinthians 10:16 NKJV), "table of the Lord" (10:21), and "Lord's supper" (11:20). The commonly used term *Eucharist* is based on the Greek word *eucharistesas* ("had given thanks") in 1 Corinthians 11:24. The traditional Roman Catholic term, the "Mass," is not based upon Scripture. It is taken from a Latin term (*missio*) that is used to dismiss the congregation in the Roman Catholic liturgy.

Jesus instituted the sacrament of the Lord's Supper during his celebration of the Passover with his disciples in the upper room (Matthew 26:26–29; Mark 14:22–25; Luke 22:14–20). According to Paul: "The Lord Jesus on the night when he was betrayed took bread, and when he had given thanks, he broke it, and said, 'This is my body which is for you. Do this in remembrance of me.' In the same way also he took the cup, after supper, saying, 'This cup is the new covenant in my blood. Do this, as often as you drink it, in remembrance of me.' For as often as you eat this bread and drink the cup, you proclaim the Lord's death until he comes" (1 Corinthians 11:23–26). Jesus intended for his people to observe this sacrament until his second advent.

The Reformed confessions, including the Westminster Confession of Faith, reject several erroneous teachings connected with the Lord's Supper (29.2–8). The Reformed confessions, for example, reject what the Roman Catholic Church refers to as the "sacrifice of the Mass." According to Rome, the Mass is a bloodless, propitiatory sacrifice. It is, in fact, said to be the same sacrifice that Christ offered on the cross (Canons and Decrees of the Council of Trent, twenty-second session, §§1–2). The Reformed confessions also reject the Roman Catholic practice of worshiping the elements of the Lord's Supper.

Historically, there have been four different ways of understanding Christ's presence in the sacrament of the Lord's Supper. The Roman Catholic understanding of Christ's presence is termed "transubstantiation." According to the Roman doctrine, when the priest speaks the words of consecration over the elements of bread and wine, a miracle occurs. The substances of the bread and the wine are said to be changed into the substance of the body and blood of Christ, while the accidents remain the same. (The term *substance* describes a thing's essential nature, while the term *accidents* describes its outward appearances.) The Lutheran understanding of Christ's presence is termed "consubstantiation" (confessing Lutherans traditionally reject the term). According to the Lutheran view, the bread and wine remain bread and wine, but Christ's body and blood are really present "in, with, and under" the bread and wine. The Zwinglian understanding of Christ's presence is best described as "symbolic memorialism." This doctrine denies any real presence of Christ in the sacrament. The sacramental elements and actions are strictly symbolic and are intended to bring to mind what Christ accomplished for believers in his death on the cross.

In contrast with these three views is the Reformed doctrine of Christ's presence. The Reformed confessions, to a greater or lesser degree, follow Calvin in teaching that Christ is truly present in the sacrament of the Lord's Supper, but not in a local or corporeal manner.[10] The Reformed understanding of the presence of Christ is based on the sacramental union between the signs and things signified. They are to be distinguished without being separated. Calvin explains:

> The godly ought by all means to keep this rule: whenever they see symbols appointed by the Lord, to think and be persuaded that the truth of the thing signified is surely present there. For why should the Lord put in your hand the symbol of his body, except to assure you of a true participation in it? But if it is true that a visible sign is given us to seal the gift of a thing invisible, when we have received the symbol of the body, let us no less surely trust that the body itself is also given to us.[11]

In the Reformed doctrine of Calvin, parallelism is at work between the action of the minister during the observance of the sacrament and the work of God. What is promised and offered through the visible sacramental signs is truly given by God to those who receive the promise in faith (Romans 2:25–29; Colossians 2:11–12). The action of God is not, however, necessarily tied to the instant of time that the visible sacrament is observed (Westminster Confession of Faith 28.6).

According to Calvin and the Reformed confessions, the means by which we partake of Christ in the Lord's Supper is faith. In contrast with the Roman doctrine, believers do not partake of the body and blood of Christ with their physical mouths. Instead we partake of Christ's body and blood by faith—the mouth of the soul. Calvin often speaks of "spiritual eating,"[12] by which he means that Christians partake of Christ's body and blood by the power of the Holy Spirit. In fact, it is only by the powerful and mysterious work of the Holy Spirit that we are able by faith to partake of the body and blood of Christ.

The Lord's Supper includes several important theological elements. Christ commanded that believers observe the Lord's Supper in "remembrance" of him; the Lord's Supper is therefore commemorative, in that it points back to Christ's sacrificial death on the cross. The Lord's Supper also points forward eschatologically; by means of the Lord's Supper, Christians proclaim the Lord's death "until he comes" (1 Corinthians 11:26), and when we partake of the Lord's Supper, we anticipate "the marriage supper of the Lamb" (Revelation 19:9). The Lord's Supper is also a visible word; when we partake of the Lord's Supper, we "proclaim the Lord's death" (1 Corinthians 11:26). Reymond explains: "The Lord's Supper itself preaches the substitutionary atonement and proclaims both the Lord's sacrificial death in our behalf and his final return to judgment."[13]

How then does the Lord's Supper function as a means of grace? Cornelis Venema explains: the Lord's Supper "serves to confirm and strengthen faith in the promises of the gospel" and also "evokes thanksgiving by *assuring* believers of their participation in Christ and his saving work."[14] The Reformed Second Helvetic Confession (1566) provides a helpful description of the Lord's Supper's function as a means of grace in a section entitled "Sacramental Eating of the Lord" (§21):

To be sure, when the believer believed, he first received the life-giving food, and still enjoys it. But therefore, when he now receives the sacrament, he does not receive nothing. For he progresses in continuing to communicate in the body and blood of the Lord, and so his faith is kindled and grows more and more, and is refreshed by spiritual food. For while we live, faith is continually increased. And he who outwardly receives the sacrament by true faith, not only receives the sign, but also, as we said, enjoys the thing itself. Moreover, he obeys the Lord's institution and commandment, and with a joyful mind gives thanks for his redemption and that of all mankind, and makes a faithful memorial to the Lord's death, and gives a witness before the Church, of whose body he is a member. Assurance is also given to those who receive the sacrament that the body of the Lord was given and his blood shed, not only for men in general, but particularly for every faithful communicant, to whom it is food and drink unto eternal life.[15]

Worthy partakers, namely, those who partake of the Lord's Supper with true faith, "receive and apply unto themselves Christ crucified, and all the benefits of his death" (Westminster Larger Catechism, A. 170).

The Lord's Supper strengthens our faith and our union with Christ, but it also has a horizontal dimension. Calvin beautifully explains why Augustine's description of the Lord's Supper as "the bond of love" is appropriate:

The Lord also intended the Supper to be a kind of exhortation for us, which can more forcefully than any other means quicken and inspire us both to purity and holiness of life, and to love, peace, and concord. For the Lord so communicates his body to us there that he is made completely one with us

151

and we with him. Now, since he has only one body, of which he makes us all partakers, it is necessary that all of us also be made one body by such participation. The bread shown in the Sacrament represents this unity. As it is made of many grains so mixed together that one cannot be distinguished from another, so it is fitting that in the same way we should be joined and bound together by such great agreement of minds that no sort of disagreement or division may intrude. I prefer to explain it in Paul's words: "The cup of blessing which we bless is a communicating of the blood of Christ; and the bread of blessing which we break is a participation in the body of Christ. . . . Therefore . . . we . . . are all one body, for we partake of one bread" [I Cor. 10:16–17; cf. Vg.]. We shall benefit very much from the Sacrament if this thought is impressed and engraved upon our minds: that none of the brethren can be injured, despised, rejected, abused, or in any way offended by us, without at the same time, injuring, despising, and abusing Christ by the wrongs we do; that we cannot disagree with our brethren without at the same time disagreeing with Christ; that we cannot love Christ without loving him in the brethren; that we ought to take the same care of our brethren's bodies as we take of our own; for they are members of our body; and that, as no part of our body is touched by any feeling of pain which is not spread among all the rest, so we ought not to allow a brother to be affected by any evil, without being touched with compassion for him. Accordingly, Augustine with good reason frequently calls this Sacrament "the bond of love."[16]

Prayer as a Means of Grace

The third means of grace mentioned in the Westminster standards is prayer. The Westminster Shorter Catechism defines prayer as "an offering up of our desires unto God, for things agreeable to his will, in the name of Christ, with confession of our sins, and thankful acknowledgement of his mercies" (A. 98). Throughout Scripture, the lives of God's people are characterized by prayer (Genesis 12:8; 1 Samuel 1:9–10; 1 Chronicles 16:8–36; Daniel 9:4–19). The Psalms are the corporate prayers of the people of God. Our Lord Jesus Christ prayed continually during his earthly ministry (Matthew 26:36–44), and he continues to make intercession for his people as our high priest (Romans 8:34). Jesus also taught his disciples that they should pray (Matthew 6:5–13).

But why? Why are Christians to pray? The Heidelberg Catechism (1563) provides an answer: "Because it is the chief part of the thankfulness which God requires of us, and because God will give his grace and Holy Spirit only to such as earnestly and without ceasing beg them from him and render thanks unto him for them" (A. 116). Our Father gives grace to those who ask. Calvin observes: "That we lie on the earth poor and famished and almost destitute of spiritual blessings, while Christ sits in glory at the right hand of the Father, clothed with the highest majesty of empire, must be imputed to our slothfulness and the narrowness of our faith."[17] We do not have because we do not ask (James 4:2; see also Matthew 6:5–13; 7:7–11; John 14:13–14; 16:23–26; 1 John 5:14–15).

Prayer also functions as a means of grace by bringing us near to God, the source of all goodness and grace. Hodge explains:

> Fellowship with Him, converse with Him, calls into exercise all gracious affections, reverence, love, gratitude, submission, faith, joy, and devotion. When the soul thus draws near to God, God draws near to it, manifests his glory, sheds abroad his love, and imparts that peace which passes all understand-

ing. Our Lord says, "If a man love me, he will keep my words: and my Father will love him, and we will come unto him, and make our abode with him" (John xiv.23). In such fellowship, the soul must be holy and must be blessed.[18]

When Moses came face to face with the Lord, his face shone (Exodus 34:29–35). When we pray, we too come into the presence of the living God. And as Paul tells us, the experience changes us: "And we all, with unveiled face, beholding the glory of the Lord, are being transformed into the same image from one degree of glory to another" (2 Corinthians 3:18). It is for this reason that Paul commands us: "Rejoice always, pray without ceasing, give thanks in all circumstances; for this is the will of God in Christ Jesus for you" (1 Thessalonians 5:16–18).

9

THE BLESSING
OF DISCIPLINE

Jerry Bridges

> But now, to the saints predestined to the kingdom of God by
> God's grace, the help of perseverance that is given is not like
> the help given to Adam. To the saints, perseverance itself is
> bestowed. They are not only given the gift by the means of
> which they can persevere; more than that, they are given the
> gift by means of which they cannot help persevering.
>
> —Augustine, *On Rebuke and Grace*

It may seem strange to include a chapter on discipline in a book
on assurance, especially a chapter entitled "The Blessing of Discipline." The subject becomes even more paradoxical when we
consider that the primary biblical text on discipline (Hebrews
12:1–11) equates discipline with the adversities of life. So, when
the author of Hebrews speaks of the discipline of the Lord in
this passage, he is actually speaking of adversity.

Everyone experiences trouble or adversity at various times and in varying degrees. It may be trivial and temporary, it may be traumatic and permanent, or it may be somewhere in between. No one, regardless of one's moral character, economic status, or station in life, escapes adversity. Eliphaz, one of Job's friends, said: "Man is born to trouble / as the sparks fly upward" (Job 5:7). It is all part of our living in a fallen and sin-cursed world.

With all this being true, is there anything particularly Christian about adversity in the life of a child of God? How can we speak of the blessing of discipline or specifically the blessing of adversity? Is not that phrase just a clever oxymoron—a sort of whistling in the dark to avoid facing the hard realities of life? And more to the point and the subject of this book, how does the discipline of adversity contribute to the assurance that one is indeed a child of God? The answers to all these questions are found in Hebrews 12:1–11:

> Therefore, since we are surrounded by so great a cloud of witnesses, let us also lay aside every weight, and sin which clings so closely, and let us run with endurance the race that is set before us, looking to Jesus, the founder and perfecter of our faith, who for the joy that was set before him endured the cross, despising the shame, and is seated at the right hand of the throne of God.
>
> Consider him who endured from sinners such hostility against himself, so that you may not grow weary or faint-hearted. In your struggle against sin you have not yet resisted to the point of shedding your blood. And have you forgotten the exhortation that addresses you as sons?
>
> "My son, do not regard lightly the discipline of the Lord, nor be weary when reproved by him.

> For the Lord disciplines the one he loves,
>> and chastises every son whom he receives."

It is for discipline that you have to endure. God is treating you as sons. For what son is there whom his father does not discipline? If you are left without discipline, in which all have participated, then you are illegitimate children and not sons. Besides this, we have had earthly fathers who disciplined us and we respected them. Shall we not much more be subject to the Father of spirits and live? For they disciplined us for a short time as it seemed best to them, but he disciplines us for our good, that we may share his holiness. For the moment all discipline seems painful rather than pleasant, but later it yields the peaceful fruit of righteousness to those who have been trained by it.

The recipients of this letter were Jewish, or Hebrew, Christians (hence the title of the letter). They were facing pressure to renounce their faith in Jesus on two fronts. First, they were being strongly reminded of the historic glories of their Jewish religion based on the law of Moses, the Aaronic priesthood, and the continual offering of the sacrifices in the temple. After all, the form of their religion was fifteen hundred years old, and it had been instituted by God himself. How could they turn away from their historic religion to worship a man who had experienced the shameful death of a Roman crucifixion?

Second, they had been experiencing significant persecution for their faith in Jesus. They had been publicly exposed to reproach and affliction, and some had suffered imprisonment and the plundering of their property (10:32–34). Apparently, those Jews who were intent on turning these believers away from their faith in Jesus and back to the historic Jewish religion not only used persuasive speech but also resorted to verbal and even physical abuse to seek to accomplish their purpose.

Try putting yourself in the shoes of those Hebrew believers. On the one hand, they were being reminded that they had turned their backs on fifteen hundred years of religion that had been instituted by God himself. On the other hand, they faced the real threat of physical and economic persecution if they continued to believe in an itinerant rabbi who ended up getting himself crucified on a Roman cross. The pressure to renounce their faith in Jesus was undoubtedly tremendous.

It is important to understand this background and context of Hebrews 12:1–11 because it helps us to see that "the discipline of the Lord" that they were experiencing and that the author of Hebrews will deal with in the passage is not the result of particular sin in their lives. Rather, it is part of God's growth process for them. This makes 12:1–11 applicable to the most godly believers today, even to those who are not wrestling with sin in their lives. It is necessary that we grasp this truth in order to understand why adversity or discipline, as the author of Hebrews calls it, should contribute to and strengthen our assurance that we are indeed children of God.

The Discipline of the Lord

In the key part of our text (12:5–11), the author uses the word *discipline* as either a noun or a verb nine times—once each in 12:5, 6, 8, 9, 11 and twice each in 12:7 and 12:10. Obviously, discipline—and more specifically "the discipline of the Lord"—is the subject of the passage. What then is the discipline of the Lord?

When we use the word *discipline* in a parent-child context, we most often mean some kind of remedial punishment, such as spanking a small child or withholding a privilege from an older child. The author of Hebrews, however, uses a word that can best be described as child training. It is the same word that the apostle Paul uses in Ephesians 6:4: "Fathers, do not provoke your children to anger, but bring them up in the *discipline* and instruction of the Lord." Perhaps the words in 2 Timothy 3:16 that describe the role of Scripture in Christian growth—teaching, reproof, correction, and training in righteousness—can help us understand all that is involved in spiritual child training.

The author of Hebrews, however, is concerned with one particular aspect of the Lord's discipline—namely, adversity in the life of the believer. Although the word *adversity* does not occur in Hebrews 12, it is implied all through the passage and is obviously to be understood that way because of the circumstances of the recipients of the letter.

We can best see this connection if we mentally insert the word *adversity* with each reference to God's discipline. For example, in Hebrews 12:6 we can mentally read: "For the Lord disciplines [through adversity] the one he loves." And in 12:10: "[Through adversity] he disciplines us for our good." Adversity then is such an important part of God's spiritual training of his children that he divinely inspired the author of Hebrews to give it fairly extensive treatment.

Adversity and Assurance

This is a book, however, on assurance and perseverance. What part then does adversity play in helping to establish our assurance that we are indeed children of God? And what part does adversity play in enabling us to persevere in the race that is set before us (12:1)?

The answer to the first question lies right on the face of the text: "The Lord disciplines the one he loves" (12:6). "God is treating you as sons" (12:7). "If you are left without discipline . . . then you are . . . not sons" (12:8). Nothing could be clearer; the discipline of adversity is a mark of being a child of God. Or to say it another way, being a child of God is always accompanied by adversity—not constant adversity, of course, but as often as the Father deems it profitable for us (12:10).

Adversity, however, is not only a mark of our being a child of God, it is also proof to us of our heavenly Father's love: "For the Lord disciplines the one he loves" (12:6). The Greek word *agapao* denotes the highest form of love. It is not the weak, shallow type of love shown by the proverbial indulgent grandparent who winks at the mischievous deeds of a grandchild. Rather, it is the love of a parent who is deeply concerned about the character of a child and is willing to administer the painful discipline necessary to build that character.

As if to reinforce this truth, the author adds in 12:6: "[He] chastises every son whom he receives." Chastisement is a severe expression of discipline. It speaks of the intensity of the pain that we often experience as part of God's disciplinary process. As I write these words, I think immediately of a young woman who for several years has experienced excruciating and uninterrupted physical pain due to a disease that does not respond to any treatment. And I think of the emotional and spiritual pain of her parents as they cry out to God for her relief without seeing any answer from him. Is this a mark of God's fatherly love? That is what the author of Hebrews tells us, and that is what the young woman and her parents cling to because they choose to believe the truth about God's sovereign love.

The Purpose of Adversity

The purpose of adversity as stated in this passage is twofold. In Hebrews 12:1, the author challenges his readers, just as he challenges us, to "lay aside every weight, and sin which clings so closely." Because the King James Version reads "the sin which doth so easily beset us," many people misunderstand what the author is saying. The expression *besetting sins* implies particular persistent sins in one's life that are difficult to deal with. This is not the intent of the author. Instead, he is referring to the very fountain of sin itself—our flesh, which clings so closely to us because it is actually in us, continually opposing the work of the Spirit in our lives (Galatians 5:17). Adversity rightly received has the effect of stripping away the expressions of the flesh in our lives.

So, one purpose of the discipline of adversity in Hebrews 12 is to deal with sin in general—that is, our sinful disposition and our continual tendency toward sin. It is true that God sometimes disciplines us because of our persistence in some particular sin. This was the case in the Corinthian church, where some were flagrantly abusing the Lord's Supper and were experiencing the Lord's discipline as a result (1 Corinthians 11:27–32). But in the absence of specific and persistent sin, we can safely say that God's discipline addresses our overall character and the need to purge our character of its sinful tendencies.

The second purpose of the discipline of adversity is "that we may share his holiness" (Hebrews 12:10). Whereas the first purpose is stated negatively—to "lay aside [get rid of] . . . [the] sin which clings so closely"—this purpose is stated positively in the sense of conforming us more and more to the holy character of God himself. This twofold purpose of adversity reflects the put-off/put-on principle of Christian growth stated by Paul in

Ephesians 4:22–24: "Put off your old self, which belongs to your former manner of life and is corrupt through deceitful desires . . . and . . . to put on the new self, created after the likeness of God in true righteousness and holiness."

Positive character traits, for the most part, can be learned only in the crucible of adversity. Consider those traits called by Paul "the fruit of the Spirit . . . love, joy, peace, patience, kindness, goodness, faithfulness, gentleness, self-control" (Galatians 5:22–23). We learn to love truly only when circumstances expose our inherent selfishness or only when we are placed in close quarters with someone who is difficult to love. We learn true joy and peace only when we experience circumstances that in themselves tend to rob us of our joy and peace in the Lord. We learn patience only by being in the continual presence of someone whose actions try our patience. We learn to trust God only when he places us in circumstances in which we are forced to depend on him. All the admirable traits of Christian character then are formed and grown through the discipline of adversity.

The wonderful assurance in all our adversities is that our loving and wise heavenly Father is administering them to us for our good. In Hebrews 12:10, the author contrasts the fallible wisdom of human parents in administering discipline with the infallible wisdom of God. He says our earthly fathers "disciplined us for a short time as it seemed best to them." All of us who are parents realize there have been times in the discipline of our children when we wrestled internally or perhaps between father and mother over the appropriate discipline in terms of type, duration, or intensity. Sometimes we second-guessed ourselves afterward simply because of our limited wisdom and parenting skills.

By contrast, the author says our Father "disciplines us for our good" (12:10). He knows exactly what discipline we need and what adversity will accomplish that purpose. He does not have to debate within himself over what is most suitable for us. Moreover, he never brings more pain than is necessary to accomplish his purpose: "For he does not willingly afflict / or grieve the children of men" (Lamentations 3:33).

Most of the time we cannot see the purpose of a particular adversity we are going through. In fact, that is part of the pain. It all seems so random and senseless. But we should be content with the knowledge that God knows what he is about and that he has a wise and loving purpose for every adverse circumstance that comes into our lives.

The author of Hebrews does not deny or minimize the pain that comes through the discipline of adversity. He is very forthright that "for the moment all discipline seems painful" (12:11). But he looks beyond the immediate pain to what he calls "the peaceful fruit of righteousness."

We may conclude that all adversity that we experience is a part of God's fatherly discipline—all, without exception. There is no such thing as chance or meaningless events in our lives. The author says: "It is for discipline that you have to endure" (12:7). Endure what? It is obvious from the context that he means to endure adversity. In effect, he is saying: "It is for the [purpose of] discipline that you have to endure [adversity]." All adversity, in whatever form and from whatever source it comes to us, is an expression of our Father's discipline.

We know that adversity comes to us in many forms and from many sources. Much of it comes from what we may call impersonal circumstances—serious illnesses, disastrous weather, or even the careless but unintentional actions of other people. Most painful of all, though, are the adversities that are the result of deliberate, and often sinful, actions of others. It may be slander that destroys our reputation, it may be that we fail to receive a well-earned promotion, or it may be the betrayal of a friend we trusted. All of us can furnish examples of the impersonal forms of adversity in our lives, and many are all too familiar with the type of adversity that comes through the sinful actions of other people.

In the case of the Hebrew Christians, their adversity was in the form of persecution and pressure because of their faith in Christ. Quite likely, some of that persecution came from within their own families. That is certainly true in many places around the world today. In fact, the adversity faced by believers in some countries because of their faith in Jesus would make many of our troubles seem incidental. But regardless of the severity and source of the adversities, all of them—whether trivial or traumatic—are part of God's discipline of us for our good.

Profiting from Adversity

The author of Hebrews, however, does more than assure us that all adversity we face is part of God's disciplinary process in our lives. He also tells us how we can align ourselves with God's purpose in discipline so as to profit by it.

In Hebrews 12:5, quoting from the book of Proverbs, the author of Hebrews exhorts us "not [to] regard lightly the discipline of the Lord." It may strike us as strange to think of making light of the Lord's discipline. I cannot think, for example, of any instance when I have regarded adversity—whether trivial or traumatic—as a light thing. But we make light of God's discipline when we fail to see God's hand in whatever adversities we encounter. Instead of acknowledging them as being from God, we tend to view them as chance circumstances and as something to be endured as quickly as possible. But the psalmist saw God's hand in all his afflictions: "It is good for me that I was afflicted, / that I might learn your statutes" (Psalm 119:71). Unlike our tendency, the psalmist saw every adversity or affliction as a means of growth in his walk with God.

The Scripture passage that helps us most in seeing every instance of adversity as being part of God's discipline in our lives is 1 Thessalonians 5:18: "Give thanks in all circumstances; for this is the will of God in Christ Jesus for you." The will of God in this passage is the moral will of God, not his providential will. This means that the giving of thanks in all circumstances, whether good or bad, is an act of obedience on our part.

To give thanks in a particular circumstance, however, requires that we first acknowledge the circumstance to be from the invisible hand of God even though the proximate cause may be the action of another person or some so-called impersonal action we often encounter. Then having acknowledged God's hand in the situation, we accept it as part of his discipline in our lives. This does not come easily for any of us. Our natural tendency, especially in the ordinary difficulties of life, is to fret and fume and to succumb to feelings of frustration. However, believing that he will use this situation for our good so that we may share in his holiness, by an act of the will we thank God for what he is doing in our lives through the particular circumstance.

The second exhortation for responding properly to God's discipline is not to grow weary under it (Hebrews 12:5). The temptation to weariness under God's discipline occurs when we experience a series of difficulties over time or else a single major adversity that never ends. At the time of his writing about it in 2 Corinthians 12, Paul had experienced the adversity of his thorn in the flesh for many years, and he expected it to last the remainder of his life. Paul was no doubt tempted to groan under his thorn because he pleaded with the Lord on three separate occasions for its removal. But apparently after that third time, he received God's assurance: "My grace is sufficient for you, for my power is made perfect in weakness" (12:9).

This is the way we can keep from growing weary under God's discipline—to rely on the sufficiency of his sustaining grace. Grace is expressed in the New Testament in a number of ways. In Paul's experience with his thorn, grace was God's power enabling him to accept, and even rejoice, in his weakness. But God's power does not just drop down from heaven. Rather, it is mediated to us by his Spirit and most often through the Scriptures. Two passages will encourage someone going through sustained trials: Hebrews 13:5 (God's promise that he "will never leave you nor forsake you") and Romans 8:38–39 (Paul's assurance that nothing, however disastrous it may be, "will be able to separate us from the love of God in Christ Jesus").

The third exhortation for responding properly to God's discipline is to submit to it (Hebrews 12:9). Negatively, this means we do not become angry at God or charge him with injustice. The statement that "it is fine to get angry with God; he's a big boy; he can handle it" is absolute blasphemy. God indeed can handle our anger, not because he is a "big boy" but because he is merciful and gracious to forgive our sin for Christ's sake. But anger against God is sin because it is charging the infinitely holy God with wrongdoing.

Short-term anger toward God may be only an emotional response to a difficult situation. But even that is a charge of injustice against God and must be repented of. More serious, however, is anger toward God that continues over a number of years because of some adversities that occurred years ago. Such an attitude amounts to a grudge against God and is actually rebellion against him.

Positively, to submit to the Lord's discipline means that we accept all adversity as coming from his loving hand for our good.

Our response then should be one of humble submission and trust, knowing that there is still much in our character that needs improving. Peter wrote: "Humble yourselves, therefore, under the mighty hand of God so that at the proper time he may exalt you" (1 Peter 5:6). This is the way we should submit to adversity.

An old quotation of unknown origin sent to me shortly after the death of my first wife has helped me respond more positively to God's discipline:

> Lord, I am willing to
>> receive what you give
>> lack what you withhold and
>> relinquish what you take.

That so beautifully expresses a positive, humble submission to God. Submission does not mean that we should not pray for relief from difficult circumstances we face or that we should not seek legitimate means to gain relief. Sometimes the discipline that God is after is the strengthening of our faith as we see his deliverance. At other times, he wants us to experience the sustaining power of his grace because the adversity does not go away.

The important thing is our attitude. We can pray earnestly to God for relief and still be submissive to him as to the outcome. Jesus is our supreme example in this as he prayed: "My Father, if it be possible, let this cup pass from me; nevertheless, not as I will, but as you will" (Matthew 26:39).

The Challenge to Perseverance

All that the author of Hebrews says to us in this passage is intended to bolster our assurance that we are children of God and

167

objects of his infinite love and care. The discipline of adversity, far from causing us to question our being a child of God, should affirm it to us since "the Lord disciplines the one he loves."

The passage, however, speaks to us not only about assurance but also about our perseverance in the faith. In Reformed theology, we have always believed that *God's preservation* of his people and *our perseverance* go hand in hand as two sides of the same coin. In fact, although the passage gives us ample ground for our assurance, the major thrust is that of perseverance. The author actually begins the passage with a challenge to run with endurance, or perseverance, the race that is set before us.

To encourage us in the race, he urges us to look to Jesus and his example of perseverance throughout his life. We know that no other human being has ever suffered the adversity that our Lord experienced. All through his life, "he was despised and rejected by men; / a man of sorrows, and acquainted with grief" (Isaiah 53:3). And even toward the end of his life, his own brothers mocked him because they did not believe in him (John 7:1–5).

The scourging and crucifixion at the hands of Roman soldiers caused physical pain far beyond what any of us can imagine. But beyond the pain was the shame of the cross. At the time Jesus lived on earth, nothing more disgraceful and shameful could happen to anyone than to suffer public crucifixion. It was a fate reserved for the worst criminals and the lowest social outcasts. It was so degrading that Roman citizens could be crucified only for great crimes, such as treason or insurrection, and then only after they had been stripped of their citizenship by flogging. There was no greater depth of shame and humiliation than what our Lord experienced as he hung on the cross. All this in spite of Jesus being the only perfectly sinless human who ever lived.

But far above all the human pain and shame that he experienced, our Lord's greatest suffering came as he endured the unmitigated wrath of God poured out on him as he stood in our place paying the penalty for our sins. One of the old hymns expressed it: "Bearing shame and scoffing rude, in my place condemned he stood."[1]

And why did he do this? Obviously, it was because of his great love for us. In fact, John wrote: "By this we know love, that he laid down his life for us" (1 John 3:16). But in Hebrews, the author says that it was "for the joy that was set before him [that he] endured the cross, despising the shame" (12:2). Jesus looked beyond the cross and saw "a great multitude that no one could number, from every nation, from all tribes and peoples and languages" that he had ransomed standing before God's throne (Revelation 7:9; see also 5:9). He looked beyond the cross to the reward of his sufferings. In his humanity, he could by faith see his beautiful bride—the church—that he purchased with his own blood. And as he kept the reward steadily in view, he was enabled to endure the pain and to despise the shame.

We, as his disciples who follow behind him, have an opportunity to follow his example, although on a much smaller scale. Paul wrote in Romans 8:18: "For I consider that the sufferings of this present time are not worth comparing with the glory that is to be revealed in us." And in 2 Corinthians 4:17 he wrote: "For this slight momentary affliction is preparing for us an eternal weight of glory beyond all comparison." However severe the discipline we face in this life, the glory that is to come will be beyond all comparison. None of us will ever say in heaven that our sufferings were not worthwhile.

To follow the example of Jesus, then, means that we keep our hearts firmly fixed on the reward—what Paul calls the "eternal weight of glory" that awaits us. What this weight of glory will look like is something unknown to us in this life. We only know that by comparison all of our adversity will seem like a "slight momentary affliction."

We may indeed speak of "the blessing of discipline," even though such discipline comes to us in the form of the adversities of this life. All of our adversities, regardless of their source and severity, come to us from the infinitely wise and loving heart of our Father, who intends them for our good. Far from causing us to doubt our salvation, the discipline of adversity should assure us that we are indeed children of the living God. Let us then in this confidence "fix . . . our eyes on Jesus" (Hebrews 12:2 NASB) and run with perseverance the race that is set before us.

Epilogue:
The Anatomy of Doubt
and Assurance

R. C. Sproul

Surely, while we teach that faith ought to be certain and assured, we cannot imagine any certainty that is not tinged with doubt, or any assurance that is not assailed by some anxiety.

—John Calvin, *Institutes of the Christian Religion*

The Rationality of Certainty

I remember our high school senior prom. The school buzzed with excitement when it was announced that live entertainment would be provided by the Smooth-Tones. The Smooth-Tones was a rhythm-and-blues singing group that made it briefly to the top of the charts with their hit record "No Doubt about It." The song celebrated the certainty that floods the heart of a boy in love.

Love—especially puppy love—admits to no uncertainty.

Few things, however, are met with such assurance and conviction. Many things that matter most to us are shrouded in the cloud of the dubious. To be sure about urgent matters, such as our health, our job security, our performance, is often a luxury that eludes us. We hope, but we are not sure.

We usually oscillate between the two poles of doubt and certainty. There are degrees of doubtfulness. I am not equally certain about everything I believe. To some questions I respond by saying: I am sure. But answers to other questions remain uncertain. The Bible itself allows for uncertainty in matters where God is silent; yet where God has spoken the matters are now certain. Nothing is more certain than that God cannot lie and cannot err. He is the basis for all genuine assurance. His Word may be attacked or denied, but never falsified.

I know of only two sources of absolute certainty: God and reason. The first source is denied by the atheist or agnostic. The second source is denied by the irrationalist. God is the source of certainty because he is the infallible source of truth. Reason yields absolute certainty in a formal way.

Rational certainty operates through logical deduction within a framework of ideas or propositions. For example, if it is true that all humans are mortal, and it is also true that Socrates is a human, then the conclusion that Socrates is mortal is absolutely certain. This certainty of reason, however, rests on a formal relationship of propositions. We may question the propositions themselves but not the validity of the conclusion.

Premises are propositions that may be true or false. Arguments are not true or false; they are valid or invalid. Logic is a tool to determine the formal validity of those arguments. Through logic we can test that validity with absolute certainty. But keep in mind the limitations of this test. The concluding premise in an argument may be true while the argument is invalid. Or the conclusion may be false while the argument is valid. For example we might argue: All fat animals are rats; Socrates is a fat animal; therefore, Socrates is a rat. Here, the argument is formally valid though the conclusion is untrue because its premises are untrue.

But why introduce questions of logic and reason into a discussion about doubt and certainty? If God says it, does not that alone remove all doubt? Certainly there is no doubt about the truth of what God says. He is an infallible source. But in making that judgment I already am using reason to banish doubt. Someone else might say: Just because God says it does not make it true. If, however, we mean by God a being who is infallible, then we can say: Indeed it does, because God is infallible, and whatever infallible beings say must be true.

Reason also enters at the level of understanding what God says. If God says, Boojiems live on Mars, I may not know what Boojiems are, but I know that they are alive and that they live on Mars. Then suppose God says, If you believe in Jesus you will be saved. My reason is involved in an attempt to understand what it means to believe, what it means to be saved, and who it is who is called Jesus.

This is simply to say that doubt and assurance are matters of the mind. My arm does not doubt anything. My foot has no convictions. My thumb understands nothing. I may have feeling in my stomach or other physical symptoms related to issues of doubt or assurance, but they flow from the mind, not apart from it. Assurance floods my heart and fills my soul only when my mind has been convinced of the truth.

This is why it is urgent that we fully apply our minds to the Word of God. Faith—and assurance—comes from hearing and hearing by the Word of God (Romans 10:17). We hear sounds with our ears. But before we can distinguish meaning, the sounds must be processed by the mind. An ear severed from the mind hears and understands nothing.

Not all our beliefs are self-evident truths. Indeed, we can rest assured that error invades our thinking at many points. If we knew which points we would dispense with error. Doubt can help lead us from error to truth. Doubt can be a vital tool for the achievement of assurance. To gain assurance of crucial truths often requires that we doubt premises that we have accepted uncritically. Doubt forces us back to first principles.

Doubt does not, indeed cannot, exist in a vacuum. Without some knowledge I cannot doubt at all. It is in the light of truth that doubt becomes a possibility. But doubt cannot ever have the last word. Only truth can establish doubt. Truth demands that we doubt what does not conform to truth.

When we build our house on truths that are sure, then we can dwell in the comfort of assurance. It is the foundation that is most crucial. Only with a sound foundation can we safely and rightly say: No doubt about it.

Skepticism in Doubt

Spiritus sanctus non est skepticus—"The Holy Spirit is not a skeptic." So Luther rebuked Erasmus of Rotterdam after Erasmus expressed disdain for Luther's statement that one could be confident in the truth of an assertion. Luther roared: "The making of assertions is the very mark of the Christian. Take away assertions and you take away Christianity. Away now with the skeptics!"[1]

Doubt is the hallmark of the skeptic. The skeptic dares to doubt the indubitable. Even demonstrable proof fails to persuade. The skeptic dwells on Mount Olympus, far aloof from the struggles of mortals who care to pursue truth. But doubt has other faces. It is the assailant of the faithful, striking fear into the hearts of the hopeful. Like Edith Bunker, doubt asks: "Are you sure? . . . Are you sure you're sure?" Doubt nags the soul. Still, doubt can appear as a servant of truth. Indeed, it is the champion of truth when it wields its sword against what is properly dubious. It is a citadel against credulity. Authentic doubt has the power to sort out and clarify the difference between the certain and the uncertain, between the genuine and the spurious.

Consider René Descartes. In his search for clear, distinct, certain ideas he employed the application of a rigorous and systematic doubt process. He endeavored to doubt everything he could possibly doubt. He doubted what he saw with his eyes and heard with his ears, for he realized that our senses can deceive us. He doubted authorities, both civil and ecclesiastical, knowing that recognized authorities can be wrong. He would submit to no *fides implicitum* claimed by any human being or institution. Biographies usually declare that Descartes was French, but his works reveal that he was surely born in Missouri.

Descartes doubted everything he could possibly doubt until he reached the point where he realized that there was one thing he could not doubt. He could not doubt that he was doubting. To doubt that he was doubting was to prove that he was doubting. No doubt about it.

From that premise of indubitable doubt, Descartes appealed to the formal certainty yielded by the laws of immediate inference. Using impeccable deduction he concluded that doubt required thought. From there it was a short step to his famous axiom: *Cogito ergo sum* ("I think, therefore I am").

At last Descartes arrived at certainty, the assurance of his own personal existence. This was, of course, before David Hume attacked causality and before Immanuel Kant argued that the self belongs to the unknowable noumenal realm that requires a "transcendental apperception" (whatever that is) to affirm at all. One wonders how Descartes would have responded to Hume and Kant had he lived long enough to deal with them. I have no doubt that the man of doubt would have prevailed.

Clearly there were unstated assumptions lurking beneath the surface of Descartes's thought processes. One assumption was the existence of logic itself. The conclusion that to doubt doubt is to prove doubt is born of logic. It assumes the validity of the law of noncontradiction. If the law of noncontradiction is not a valid and necessary law of thought, then one could argue (irrationally) that doubt can be doubt and not be doubt at the same time and in the same relationship.

The second assumption was the validity of the law of causality, which is merely an extension of the law of noncontradiction. Descartes could not doubt that an effect *must* have an antecedent cause. Doubt, by logical necessity, requires a doubter, even as thought requires a thinker. This is simply arguing that no action of any kind can proceed from nonbeing. Hume's skepticism of causality was cogent insofar as he brilliantly displayed the difficulty of assigning a particular cause to a particular effect or event. But not even Hume was able to repeal the law of causality itself. It is one thing to doubt what the cause of a particular effect is; it is quite another to argue that the effect may have no cause at all.

Countless thinkers have made this error since Hume. In a critical review of my book *Classical Apologetics*, the able and thoroughly Christian reviewer observed: "The problem with Sproul is that he refuses to acknowledge the possibility of an uncaused effect." I wrote to my reviewing colleague and pleaded guilty to the charge. *Mea culpa.* I do refuse to acknowledge even the most remote possibility of an uncaused effect. I have the same obstreperous stubbornness regarding circles that are not round and married bachelors. I asked my friend to cite one example, real or theoretical, of an uncaused effect and I would repent in dust and ashes. I am still waiting for his reply—either to deliver the goods or admit his glaring error.

I certainly allow for an uncaused being, namely God, but not for uncaused effects. An uncaused effect is an oxymoron, a veritable contradiction in terms, a statement so patently and analytically false that Descartes could refute it in his Dutch oven without the benefit of empirical testing.

So how does this affect the Christian who struggles with the doubts that assail faith? The content of Christianity, in all its parts, cannot be reduced simplistically to Cartesian syllogisms. The lesson we learn from Descartes is this: When assailed by doubt it is time to search diligently for first principles that are certain. We build upon the foundation of what is sure.

This search is a matter of consequence that affects the whole structure of apologetics. It seems astonishing that anybody would go to the extremes that Descartes insisted on, simply to discover that he existed. What could be more self-evident to a conscious being than one's own self-consciousness? But Descartes was not on a fool's errand. In a world of sophisticated skepticism Descartes sought to establish a foundation of certainty that could uphold much more than one proposition. He moved from the certitude of self-consciousness to the certitude of the existence of God—no small matter for the doubt-ridden believer. Descartes and others like him understood that one must prove the existence of God before affirming the trustworthiness of Scripture and the birth and work of the person of Christ. Once it is certain that God exists and reveals himself in Scripture, there is ground for a legitimate *fides implicitum*.

But the order of the process used to destroy doubt is crucial. For example, the miracles of the Bible cannot prove, and were never designed to prove, the existence of God. The very possibility of a miracle requires that there first be a God who can empower it. It is not the Bible that proves the existence of God; it is God who, through miracle, attests that the Bible is his Word. Once the necessity of a self-revealing God is proven, belief in the Bible becomes implicitly a virtue.

The most important certainty we can ever have is the foundational certainty of the existence of God. It is this matter that prompted Edwards to declare: "Nothing is more certain than that there must be an unmade and unlimited being."[2]

On this bedrock of certainty rests the promises of that unmade, unlimited being. On these premises we rest our faith. Doubting served Descartes well, but Edwards knew that ultimately it is dubious to doubt the indubitable.

The Joy of Assurance

After Blaise Pascal died in 1662 his servant discovered a small piece of parchment sewn into the doublet that belonged to the mathematician and Christian thinker. At the top of the paper Pascal had drawn a cross. Beneath the cross were these words:

> The year of grace 1654
> Monday 23 November
> . . . From about half past ten in the evening until half
>   past midnight.

Fire

"God of Abraham, God of Isaac, God of Jacob" (Exodus
  3:6), not of philosophers and scholars.

Certainty, certainty, heartfelt, joy, peace.
  God of Jesus Christ.
  God of Jesus Christ.
  My God and your God (John 20:17).
  "Thy God shall be my God" (Ruth 1:16).
  The world forgotten, and everything except God.
  He can only be found in the ways taught in the Gospels.
  Greatness of the human soul.
  "O righteous Father, the world had not known thee,
    but I have known thee" (John 17:25).
  Joy, joy, joy, tears of joy.
  I have cut myself off from him.
  They have forsaken me, the fountain of living waters
    (Jeremiah 2:13).
  "My God wilt thou forsake me?" (cf. Matthew 27:46).
  Let me not be cut off from him forever!
  "And this is life eternal, that they might know thee,
    the only true God, and Jesus Christ whom thou
    hast sent" (John 17:3).
  Jesus Christ.
  Jesus Christ.
  I have cut myself off from him, shunned him, denied
    him, crucified him.
  Let me never be cut off from him!
  He can only be kept by the ways taught in the Gospel.
  Sweet and total renunciation.
  Total submission to Jesus Christ and my director.
  Everlasting joy in return for one day's effort on earth.
  I will not forget thy word (Psalm 119:16).
  Amen.[3]

Pascal's "night of fire" was an experience that gripped his soul and changed the course of his life. He kept the record of it literally close to his heart. The resounding theme of his record was one of joy—a sublime joy accompanied by peace. Coupled to his echo of joy is the word *certainty*. His sublime joy was linked inseparably to some kind of assurance. Joy is the result of assurance. It is the assurance, not merely of God's existence that yields such joy, but his divine favor and compassion. To know that we are his is the rock upon which sublime joy rests.

A "night of fire" settled something in Pascal's soul, once and for all time. To gain assurance of our redemption is to get our lives settled. Once assurance is attained, doubt exits from the soul—and joy rushes in to fill the vacuum.

It is a quest worth the journey.

NOTES

Preface

1. J. C. Ryle, *Holiness: Its Nature, Hindrances, Difficulties, and Roots* (repr. Moscow, ID: Nolan, 2001), 121.

Chapter 1: Our Sure Foundation

1. John Piper, *Desiring God* (Sisters, OR: Multnomah, 1986), 130.

2. Patrick Morley, *The Man in the Mirror* (Grand Rapids: Zondervan, 1997), 60.

3. Francis A. Schaeffer, *The Church at the End of the Twentieth Century* (Downers Grove, IL: InterVarsity, 1970), 129.

4. Sinclair B. Ferguson, *The Holy Spirit* (Contours of Christian Theology; Downers Grove, Il: InterVarsity, 1996), 13.

5. John MacArthur, *The Gospel according to Jesus* (rev. ed.; Grand Rapids: Zondervan, 1994), 113–14.

6. John Murray, *Redemption Accomplished and Applied* (Grand Rapids: Eerdmans, 1955), 68–69.

7. John Calvin, *Commentary on the Book of Psalms* (trans. James Anderson; repr. Grand Rapids: Baker, 2003), 2.388.

Chapter 2: Assured from Beginning to End

1. This essay adapted with permission from Philip Graham Ryken, *The Message of Salvation* (The Bible Speaks Today; Downers Grove, IL: InterVarsity/Leicester: Inter-Varsity, 2001).

2. John Calvin, *Institutes of the Christian Religion* (ed. John T. McNeill; trans. Ford Lewis Battles; Library of Christian Classics 20–21; Philadelphia: Westminster, 1960), 3.24.5.

3. John Calvin, *Commentary on the Epistles of Paul to the Galatians and Ephesians* (trans. William Pringle; repr. Grand Rapids: Baker, 2003), 208.

Chapter 3: Guarded through Faith

1. Martin Luther, *Luther's Works*, vol. 4: *Lectures on Genesis, chaps. 21–25* (ed. Jaroslav Pelikan; St. Louis: Concordia, 1964), 145.

2. John Calvin, *Romans and Thessalonians* (trans. Ross Mackenzie; Grand Rapids: Eerdmans, 1995), 370.

3. John Calvin's commentary on Psalms, cited in Graham Miller, *Calvin's Wisdom* (Edinburgh: Banner of Truth, 1992), 10.

4. Thomas Schreiner and Ardel B. Caneday, *The Race Set before Us: A Biblical Theology of Perseverance and Assurance* (Downers Grove, IL: Inter-Varsity, 2001).

5. I. Howard Marshall, *Kept by the Power of God: A Study of Perseverance and Falling Away* (repr. Minneapolis: Bethany Fellowship, 1974).

6. R. T. Kendall, *Once Saved, Always Saved* (Chicago: Moody, 1983); and Zane C. Hodges, *The Gospel under Siege: A Study on Faith and Works* (2nd ed.; Dallas: Rendencion Viva, 1991).

7. R. C. Sproul, *Chosen by God* (Wheaton: Tyndale, 1986), 177.

Chapter 4: Assured in Christ

1. Cited from John E. Marshall, "Rabbi Duncan and the Problem of Assurance," in *Life and Writings* (Edinburgh: Banner of Truth, 2005), 207.

2. John Murray, "The Assurance of Faith," in *Collected Writings of John Murray* (Edinburgh: Banner of Truth, 1977), 2.264–74.

3. It is not surprising that the extensive and well-indexed *Catechism of the Catholic Church* (New York: Doubleday, 1995) contains no reference to assurance of salvation.

4. Murray, "Assurance of Faith," 266–67.

5. John Murray, *Redemption Accomplished and Applied* (Grand Rapids: Eerdmans, 1955), 43.

6. James Montgomery Boice, *Foundations of the Christian Faith* (Downers Grove, IL: InterVarsity, 1986), 324.

7. Charles Hodge, *Systematic Theology* (repr. Grand Rapids: Eerdmans, 1993), 2.545.

8. J. I. Packer, "Introduction," in John Owen's *The Death of Death in the Death of Christ* (Edinburgh: Banner of Truth, 1989), 7.

9. Hodge, *Systematic Theology*, 2.482.

10. This does not deny, however, that Christ's offer of salvation is sincerely presented to all the world. The free offer of the gospel to all is one of the designed effects of the cross. In 1583 Calvin could say that God's love "extends to all men, inasmuch as Christ Jesus reaches out his arms to call and allure all men both great and small, and to win them to him"; *Sermons on Deuteronomy* (repr. Edinburgh: Banner of Truth, 1989), 423. It is in this restricted sense that we may speak of God's saving love for all the world.

11. Iain H. Murray, *The Old Evangelicalism: Old Truths for a New Awakening* (Edinburgh: Banner of Truth, 2005), 119.

12. Murray, *Redemption Accomplished and Applied*, 106.

13. Ibid., 111.

14. R. L. Dabney, *Systematic Theology* (repr. Edinburgh: Banner of Truth, 1985), 710

15. Marshall, "Rabbi Duncan and the Problem of Assurance," 230.

16. Murray, "Assurance of Faith," 271.

17. J. C. Ryle, *Holiness: Its Nature, Hindrances, Difficulties, and Roots* (repr. Durham, UK: Evangelical Press, 1979), 113.

18. Boice, *Foundations of the Christian Faith*, 436.

19. Ryle, *Holiness*, 115.

20. Donald Macleod, *A Faith to Live By* (Ross-shire, UK: Christian Focus, 1998), 187.

21. Ryle, *Holiness*, 114.

22. Murray, "Assurance of Faith," 274.

Chapter 5: Assurance Justified

1. There is today a considerable debate, which began in scholarly circles but has since spread, over the question of the precise significance of "justify." A number of scholars argue that the justified are simply those who belong to the covenant community. In other words justification language refers not to how we "get into" fellowship with God but rather describes those who "are in" such fellowship. It therefore belongs to the doctrine of the church (ecclesiology), not to the doctrine of how we become Christians (soteriology). The problem that ought to be obvious with this perspective is that it confuses the description of a valid consequence with the explanation of its cause. To say that

"to be justified" means "to belong to the community" sheds no more light on the exact meaning of the term than, for example, to say that "to be adopted or reconciled or regenerated" means "to belong to the community." Unless these terms have no specific denotation, each one refers to how this comes about; they are not amorphous metaphors all denoting the same thing. While they all refer to the reality of our coming into fellowship with God and his people, they each nuance a different aspect of how this takes place and what the result is. The older understanding rightly safeguarded this nuance.

2. From the hymn "Hallelujah, What a Savior!" by Philip Bliss.

3. John Calvin, *Institutes of the Christian Religion* (ed. John T. McNeill; trans. Ford Lewis Battles; Library of Christian Classics 20–21; Philadelphia: Westminster, 1960), 3.1.1.

4. Ibid.

5. John Calvin, *Romans and Thessalonians* (trans. Ross Mackenzie; Grand Rapids: Eerdmans, 1991), 167.

6. John Murray, *Redemption Accomplished and Applied* (Grand Rapids: Eerdmans, 1955/Edinburgh: Banner of Truth, 1961), 131.

7. Calvin, *Institutes of the Christian Religion*, 3.11.20.

8. Oscar Cullmann, *Christ and Time* (trans. F. V. Filson; London: SCM, 1951), 84.

9. Philip Schaff, *The Creeds of Christendom* (New York: Harper, 1877), 2.99.

10. From the well-known hymn by Frances Jane Van Alstyne (Fanny Crosby), the hymn writer who lost her sight when she was six weeks old.

Chapter 6: The Fullness of Grace

1. James W. Alexander, *Consolation to the Suffering People of God* (repr. Orlando: Soli Deo Gloria Publishers/Ligonier Ministries, 1992), 138.

2. J. C. Ryle, *Holiness: Its Nature, Hindrances, Difficulties, and Roots* (repr. Moscow, ID: Nolan, 2001), 135–36.

3. Robert Letham, "Saving Faith and Assurance in Reformed Theology: Zwingli to the Synod of Dort" (PhD thesis, University of Aberdeen, 1979).

4. Geerhardus Vos, *Biblical Theology* (repr. Edinburgh: Banner of Truth, 1996), 83–84.

5. B. B. Warfield, *Biblical Doctrines* (Edinburgh: Banner of Truth, 1929), 489–90.

Chapter 7: The Glory of True Repentance

1. Jürgen Goetzmann, in *The New International Dictionary of New Testament Theology* (ed. Colin Brown; Grand Rapids: Zondervan, 1975), 1.358.

2. J. Behm, in *Theological Dictionary of the New Testament* (ed. Gerhard Kittel; trans. Geoffrey W. Bromiley; Grand Rapids: Eerdmans, 1967), 4.1002.

3. Joseph Henry Thayer, *Greek-English Lexicon of the New Testament* (repr. Grand Rapids: Zondervan, 1962), 406.

4. Geerhardus Vos, *The Kingdom of God and the Church* (Nutley, NJ: Presbyterian & Reformed, 1972), 92–93.

5. John Owen, *The Works of John Owen* (repr. London: Banner of Truth, 1966), 6.605.

6. Ibid., 6.549.

Chapter 8: God's Means of Assurance

1. Louis Berkhof, *Systematic Theology* (Grand Rapids: Eerdmans, 1941), 604–5; Charles Hodge, *Systematic Theology* (repr. Grand Rapids: Eerdmans, 1989), 3.466.

2. John Calvin, *Institutes of the Christian Religion* (ed. John T. McNeill; trans. Ford Lewis Battles; Library of Christian Classics 20–21; Philadelphia: Westminster, 1960), 4.1.1.

3. Hodge, *Systematic Theology*, 3.478–79.

4. John Calvin, "Short Treatise on the Lord's Supper," in *Treatises on the Sacraments* (trans. Henry Beveridge; Fearn, UK: Christian Focus, 2002), 165–66.

5. Robert L. Reymond, *A New Systematic Theology of the Christian Faith* (Nashville: Nelson, 1998), 916; see also Hodge, *Systematic Theology*, 3.479–85.

6. For a helpful survey of what the Reformed confessions teach regarding the sacraments in general and baptism in particular, see Cornelis P. Venema, "The Doctrine of the Sacraments and Baptism according to the Reformed Confessions," *Mid-America Journal of Theology* 11 (2000): 21–86.

7. See *Catechism of the Catholic Church* (New York: Doubleday, 1995), §1084.

8. Reymond, *New Systematic Theology*, 922.

9. For a helpful survey of what the Reformed confessions teach regarding the Lord's Supper, see Cornelis P. Venema, "The Doctrine of the Lord's Supper in the Reformed Confessions," *Mid-America Journal of Theology* 12 (2001): 81–145.

10. For an explanation and defense of Calvin's doctrine of the Lord's Supper, see my *Given for You: Reclaiming Calvin's Doctrine of the Lord's Supper* (Phillipsburg, NJ: P&R, 2002); see also Calvin, "Short Treatise on the Lord's Supper," 163–98; idem, *Institutes of the Christian Religion*, 4.17.

11. Calvin, *Institutes of the Christian Religion*, 4.17.10.

12. Calvin, "Short Treatise on the Lord's Supper," 577–78.

13. Reymond, *New Systematic Theology*, 967.

14. Venema, "Doctrine of the Lord's Supper," 134.

15. Quoted from Arthur C. Cochrane, ed., *Reformed Confessions of the Sixteenth Century* (Louisville: Westminster, 2003), 286.

16. Calvin, *Institutes of the Christian Religion*, 4.17.38.

17. Cited in Reymond, *New Systematic Theology*, 973.

18. Hodge, *Systematic Theology*, 3.708.

Chapter 9: The Blessing of Discipline

1. From the hymn "Hallelujah, What a Savior!" by Philip Bliss.

Epilogue: The Anatomy of Doubt and Assurance

1. Martin Luther, *The Bondage of the Will* (trans. J. I. Packer and O. R. Johnston; repr. Grand Rapids: Revell, 1990), 44.

2. Jonathan Edwards, *The Miscellanies* (ed. Douglas A. Sweeney; New Haven: Yale University Press, 2004), 371 §1340.

3. Blaise Pascal, *Pensées* (trans. A. J. Krailsheimer; London: Penguin, 1995), 285–86.

Study Questions

Chapter 1: Our Sure Foundation

1. How does God use his Word to assure us of our salvation? (pp. 22–23)
2. What should be the goal of our study of God and our service to God? (pp. 24–25)
3. In our salvation, do we accept God or does he accept us? Explain. (pp. 27–29)
4. In what ways is Jesus the author and finisher of our faith? (pp. 30–31)

Chapter 2: Assured from Beginning to End

1. What is the role of the Holy Spirit in guaranteeing our salvation in Christ? (pp. 40–41)
2. Can a Christian have assurance that he or she is among God's elect? (p. 45)
3. In the ancient world seals were used to mark official documents. How does the concept of the ancient use of a seal help us understand the way God seals us by the Holy Spirit? (pp. 48–49)
4. What are some ways the Holy Spirit assures us that our faith is authentic? (p. 50)

Chapter 3: Guarded through Faith

1. In what three ways can a new believer gain a fuller assurance of his or her salvation? (p. 58)
2. Explain the "test of genuineness" view of the warnings in the book of Hebrews. (p. 61)
3. Why is the phrase "once saved, always saved" misleading? (p. 64)
4. According to R. C. Sproul, what is the only reason we are able to persevere in the faith? (p. 65)

Chapter 4: Assured in Christ

1. Why don't Roman Catholics generally pursue assurance of salvation? (p. 71)
2. Was Christ's atonement effectual? Explain. (pp. 73–75)
3. In what ways does Jesus's high priestly prayer in John 17 confirm that Jesus died for his people particularly? (p. 76)
4. What are the three biblical tests of faith the apostle John presents in his first epistle? (pp. 82–84)

Chapter 5: Assurance Justified

1. Why is the use of the word *justify* a statement about a person's status before God? (pp. 88–89)
2. In what ways is Jesus the second and last Adam? (pp. 91–92)
3. Why is faith the appropriate instrument in justification? (pp. 93–94)
4. In what ways are our hearts enlarged by grace through the assurance of faith? Explain. (pp. 104–5)

Chapter 6: The Fullness of Grace

1. What are the five reasons for seeking to grow in assurance? Explain. (pp. 109–11)

2. How does our assurance of faith affect our Christian service? (p. 110)

3. In what ways was the Old Testament believer's assurance a present reality, and in what ways was the Old Testament believer's assurance future oriented? (pp. 112–15)

4. How were Old Testament believers justified before God? (pp. 121–23)

Chapter 7: The Glory of True Repentance

1. Why is a correct understanding of repentance necessary for possessing genuine assurance? (pp. 126–28)

2. When the New Testament uses the word *repentance*, how is it to be understood? (pp. 128–29)

3. In what way is repentance a gift from God? (p. 131)

4. What kind of evidence substantiates authentic repentance? (pp. 133–36)

Chapter 8: God's Means of Assurance

1. What are the means of grace that God has established for his people? (p. 139)

2. How is the Word of God a means of grace? (pp. 140–43)

3. What does baptism signify? (p. 146)

4. What is the means by which believers partake of Christ in the Lord's Supper? Why is that significant for a believer's assurance? (pp. 150–52)

Chapter 9: The Blessing of Discipline

1. How does God use adversity in our lives to help assure us that we are his children? (p. 159)

2. What is one way through which God demonstrates his love for us as his children? Why is that significant for a believer's assurance? (p. 162)

3. What can we learn from the adversity that God brings into our lives? (pp. 164–65)

4. How should we respond to God when he allows us to face adversity? (pp. 166–67)

Epilogue: The Anatomy of Doubt and Assurance

1. Why is it important that we fully apply our minds to the Word of God in understanding what it teaches about assurance? (pp. 172–74)

2. What is the hallmark of a skeptic? Explain. (p. 175)

3. Why is an uncaused effect an oxymoron? (p. 177)

4. In what ways are joy and assurance inseparable?

INDEX OF SCRIPTURE

1:19–20 59
2:3 27
3:16 90

2 Timothy
2:12 21
2:25 33, 131
3:14–17 141
3:16 159
4:7–8 117, 118
4:10 59
4:14 118
4:18 55

Hebrews
1:1–2 115
1:1–3 119
1:4–14 119
2:10 30
2:14–17 74
3:1–6 119
4:12 141
5:1–10 119
6 60, 63
6:4 63
6:4–8 60
6:7–8 63
6:9 119
7:1–28 119
9:1–10:18 119
9:11–14 34
9:28 74
10:19–22 119
10:19–25 35
10:21–22 66
10:22 55, 120, 135
10:23 21, 55
10:32–34 157
10:39–12:2 114
11 112
11:1 111

11:8–19 112
12 159, 161
12:1 20–21, 159, 161
12:1–11 155, 156, 158
12:2 169, 170, 30
12:4 32, 33
12:5 158, 164, 165
12:5–6 36
12:5–11 158
12:6 158, 159, 160
12:7 158, 160, 163
12:8 158, 160
12:9 158, 166
12:10 158, 159, 160, 161, 162
12:11 158, 163
12:28 27
13:5 166

James
1:4 119
1:5–8 119
1:12 119
1:22–25 143
2 96
2:14 96, 97
2:17 96
2:18 96
2:18–26 119
2:20 96
2:22 96
2:23 96
2:24 96
2:26 96, 133
4:2 153
5:16 89

1 Peter
1:3 67
1:3–12 120

1:4–5 67
1:18–19 75
2:2 142
2:5 27
2:8 45
2:9 27
4:12–14 120
5:6 167

2 Peter
1:3–4 120
1:8 36
1:8–9 59
1:10 45, 59, 120
1:10–11 7

1 John
1:4 84
1:7 75, 120
1:8 136
1:9 33, 138
1:10 136
2:1 136, 138
2:2 136
2:3 120
2:3–6 83, 117, 136
2:4–6 83
2:5 120
2:15–17 117
2:18–27 82
2:21–28 136
2:22–23 82
2:23 120
2:27 120
2:29 137
3:1 36
3:1–10 136
3:3 111
3:4–10 83, 117
3:8 137
3:9 137

195

Index of Subjects

HIM WE PROCLAIM

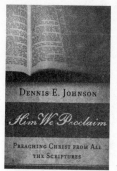

Him We Proclaim makes the hermeneutical and historical case for a return to apostolic preaching—preaching that is Christ-centered, redemptive-historical, missiologically communicated, and grounded in grace. Dennis Johnson provides examples of how this method applies to all Old and New Testament genres.

"Holds the promise of the recovery of biblical preaching for those who will give themselves to the demanding and glorious task of setting each text within the context of God's redemptive plan. This is a book that belongs on every preacher's bookshelf." —**R. Albert Mohler Jr.**

Dennis E. Johnson, 512 pp, $24.99, Paper, 978-1-59638-054-7

HOW JESUS TRANSFORMS THE TEN COMMANDMENTS

Edmund Clowney explains how Jesus intensifies the law and expands its scope to every situation in life. Going further, Clowney finds Christ in the law and shows how he fulfills it for his people. Both God's character and the gospel of Christ come into sharper focus.

"Clowney writes simply, but profoundly. Nobody had a deeper understanding of how all Scripture witnesses to Christ. I highly recommend this book for adult classes in churches, and for all who seek a better knowledge of the Lord Jesus." —**John M. Frame**

Edmund P. Clowney, 176 pp, $12.99, Paper, 978-1-59638-036-3

P U B L I S H I N G
P.O. BOX 817 • PHILLIPSBURG • NEW JERSEY 08865-0817